*The SHIFT* is a must-read for all of us in leadership. Pastor Moore has articulated the environment of change by both experiencing it and sharing it with us. He reminds us, through the valley of dry bones, that discouragement and lifelessness are not the end of the story. Yes, there is a shift, and these bones can live again. This message is not theory; it is truth born out of real struggle, prayer, and perseverance. What Pastor Moore has given us is more than a book. It is a lifeline, a prophetic word that breathes fresh hope into leaders, pastors, and visionaries who may feel as though they are standing in a valley of what used to be.

—MARK CARVER
Arkansas Administrative Bishop

*The SHIFT* is a timely call for leaders ready to move from maintenance to momentum. Johnny Moore blends biblical insight with practical wisdom to show how divine change can transform churches, organizations, and lives. This book will stir your faith and ignite vision for what's possible when God shifts everything.

—MARTIJN VAN TILBORGH
Four Rivers Media, Sanford, FL

## What people are saying about
# THE SHIFT

The power of a short phrase, *The SHIFT,* can significantly revolutionize the ministry of any local church! Not just any shift, but a divine shift that has the potential to bring vibrant, transformative change. Pastor Johnny Moore distills practical principles predicated on the acrostic S.H.I.F.T. (Spiritual life, Hospitality, Interdependence, Focus-out, and Transformation), saturated with scriptural foundation and practical experience. Pastor Moore clearly presents a process with proven components to effect transformation in one's ministry, church, or business. A great resource and a must-read for the leader who has a vision to witness a *SHIFT* and maximize their God-called destiny.

**—MICHAEL L. BAKER**
Chancellor of Education
President, Pentecostal Theological Seminary

Johnny Moore's new book, *The SHIFT,* is written in a warm and accessible style, drawing on years of experience. There is a great need for church revitalization. Johnny writes from a passion for revival and a plan for revitalization. This book is filled with practical wisdom, insights, and step-by-step plans. *The SHIFT* begins within us as leaders; we partner with God in prayer and devotion, then roll up our sleeves and lead well with a good plan. *The SHIFT* will help you do just that!!

**—DAN REILAND**
Author, leadership coach, church strategist
https://danreiland.com

Once again, Johnny Moore has demonstrated his giftings in resourcing pastors. With the release of *The SHIFT*, he draws from his years of effective pastoring to equip and encourage those in all stages of ministry.

—GARY LEWIS
General Overseer, Church of God, Cleveland, TN

SHIFTS are different! Sudden. Unplanned. Change. Directional. Accelerated. Pivots. You get the idea. Shifts are never the challenge. They happen. Shifting with shifts during the lifetime of the shift—that is the challenge. In his latest book, The SHIFT, my friend Johnny Moore will be your guide, urging you to shift.

—SAM CHAND
Leadership consultant and author of Leadership Pain

Pastor Johnny Moore has a prophetic word for every pastor with ears to hear. God wants to SHIFT the church where you pastor to a new level of effectiveness in reaching the harvest. The great thing is that Pastor Moore provides the nuts and bolts of how to obtain this SHIFT, as well as what can take place in a local church given completely to following the Spirit with passion. Read this book with a sensitive ear to the Holy Spirit and watch as He guides you to a greater harvest than you have ever imagined!

—TOBY S. MORGAN
South Carolina Church of God Executive Office

"Great pastors don't build great churches; great pastors build great people, and great people build great churches." These words, spoken by Dr. Jack Hyles fifty-three years ago, best describe The SHIFT. It is not just about church growth; it is about people growth, producing disciples of Christ building churches. I have read it—written where theory meets practice by an experienced church builder. Johnny Moore, you have done it! The SHIFT will transform people, and people will transform your church.

—RAYMOND F. CULPEPPER, D.D.
Executive Director Church of God
Division of Care, Cleveland, TN

I am thrilled to endorse my dear friend's new book, *The SHIFT: Creating an Environment for Transformation.* Written with the compassion and insight of a shepherd, Pastor Moore beautifully outlines and explains the intentional efforts required to transcend the status quo and reach the apex of revitalizing transformation. This is a must-read for anyone seeking to deepen their personal walk with Christ and facilitate impactful change and transformation in their church, their place of business, and their community.

—**M. THOMAS PROPES, D.D.**
General Director, Church of God World Missions, Cleveland, TN

One of the most frustrating things in life for me is to see things that are supposed to be moving standing still. Freeways, escalators . . . even people. In his incredible new book, *The SHIFT,* Pastor Johnny Moore not only shows us but challenges all of us to get ready for the shifting of God. Remember, the steps of a good man are ordered by the Lord.

—**BISHOP CLINT BROWN**
Judah Church, Orlando, FL

For decades, Johnny Moore has had a passion for encouraging pastors and leaders to strive for excellence in discipleship and ministry. Moore understands that the only way a church grows is when the people grow. This book is his latest attempt to encourage believers to experience the redemptive lift that comes when we give ourselves fully to the lordship of Jesus Christ. The *SHIFT* comes when we faithfully envision the mission of God!

—**DAN TOMBERLIN, DMIN, THM**
Assistant Professor of Practical Theology
Pentecostal Theological Seminary

In *The SHIFT,* Pastor Johnny Moore has given the church a true master class on revitalization. He doesn't just offer theories—he lays out practical, biblical steps for restoring health and momentum by focusing on what really matters: spiritual disciplines, discipleship, hospitality, and how we treat people. Every pastor who desires to see their church renewed should read and apply this book.

—MIKE SANES
Lead Pastor, The Harbor, Kingsland, GA

This captivating book takes the reader on a powerful journey of true revitalization. Pastor Johnny Moore lays out before us a step-by-step process that begins with your heart and ends with your harvest! This book will challenge the reader to look through Kingdom eyes, embrace the shift that is coming, and become mission-minded and vision-driven.

—PASTOR MATT WOODS
Reviving Hope, Potosi, MO

I wholeheartedly recommend *The SHIFT* by Pastor Johnny Moore to every pastor, leader, and believer longing to see God's people renewed, revived, and released into their full Kingdom potential. With the heart of a shepherd and the insight of a seasoned leader, Johnny weaves biblical truth, personal testimony, and practical strategy to show how a divine *SHIFT* can transform a church, a community, and a life.

—ROB BAILEY
State Administrative Bishop, Church of God in TX

*The SHIFT: Creating an Environment for Transformation* is a timely and Spirit-led resource for pastors and churches who are serious about cultivating genuine transformation. With clarity and wisdom, Pastor Johnny Moore guides leaders through the practical framework of relevant change. This book has the potential to serve as a blueprint for building Christ-centered communities that grow deeper, stronger, and more impactful. Every chapter challenges us to move beyond business-as-usual ministry and into intentional environments where God's power can truly change lives. I highly recommend this book to every pastor, ministry leader, and congregation that is hungry for more of God and longing to see lasting fruit.

—ISRAEL AARON COWART
Live Oak Church, Hinesville, GA

In ministry, two vital elements are essential for success: God's direction and God's timing. In his book, *The SHIFT*, Pastor Johnny Moore provides critical insight on how to discover God's direction for church growth and, just as importantly, how to implement that plan at the right time. This resource is more than theory; it's a practical guide designed to help pastors and church leaders identify the true needs of their local congregation and take actionable steps toward Spirit-led growth. Pastor Moore's "plug and play" approach empowers not only lead pastors but also equips team members to engage in the mission of reaching the lost. With wisdom born of years in ministry leadership, he offers proven formulas, assessment tools, and a roadmap that produces real results. *The SHIFT* challenges us to move from internal maintenance to external mission—a timely call to action for churches ready to impact their world for Christ.

—DERWOOD L. PERKINS, PHD
Ohio Administrative Bishop

Every day, change is happening around us. Some accept, adapt, and achieve, but many cower in self-doubt and retreat to the familiar safe haven of regular and routine. In his new book, *The SHIFT*, Pastor Johnny Moore encourages the body to stand up tall and accept the call to live not only in the environment of change but also to realize that God is demanding that we rule, rejoice, and represent. Your bones will live because the blood still works. Grab your notepad, pull out your Bible, and hold on, because you are not only going to be informed but transformed. God's not just shaking you; He is shifting you.

—ANTHONY PELT
Administrative Bishop, FL-Cocoa Church of God

First Corinthians 6:3 reveals that while one person plants a seed, and another gives it water, it is God who ultimately gives the increase, and a harvest is realized. This analogy shows us that much of what we learn from nature applies to the church. In order for both an earthly harvest and a spiritual harvest to flourish, a healthy environment is required. The ideal environment goes beyond the dimensions of the building and its physical location while encompassing aspects of community, spiritual nourishment, and outreach. In his book, *The SHIFT*, Pastor Johnny Moore offers practical and proven insights to help you cultivate and realize an abundant harvest by developing the right environment.

—**TIM HILL**
Tennessee Administrative Bishop

Making a "shift" personally or corporately is something many leaders discuss but few achieve. Having a fresh vision and mobilizing a group of followers is a task, especially when cultural norms would keep most leaders from even daring to try. Not Johnny and Dianne Moore. Believing God for what He placed in their hearts, they have spent a lifetime investing and shifting the culture in Cairo, Georgia, to develop a strong, vibrant kingdom church for their community and beyond. The principles noted in this book are tried and proven. I encourage you to read *The SHIFT*, and to *make* a "shift," as well.

—**THOMAS A. MADDEN**
Secretary General, Churches of God

Pastor Johnny is a gifted teacher and author whose books give spiritual, yet practical guidance to pastors and churches praying for a move of God. After reading it, I know *The SHIFT* is going to bless you, your church, and your community. Pick it up, read it, and put it to work!

—**PASTOR TOMMY ODUM**
The Well, Centerville, GA

# THE
# SHIFT

Copyright © 2025 by Johnny Moore

Published by AVAIL

All rights reserved. No portion of this book may be reproduced, stored in a retrieval system, or transmitted in any form or by any means—electronic, mechanical, photocopy, recording, scanning, or other—except for brief quotations in critical reviews or articles, without prior written permission of the author.

Unless otherwise specified, all scripture quotations are taken from the New American Standard Bible 1995, New American Standard Bible®, Copyright © 1960, 1971, 1977, 1995 by The Lockman Foundation. All rights reserved. Scripture quotations marked AMPC are taken from the Amplified Bible, Classic Edition, Copyright © 1954, 1958, 1964, 1965, 1987 by The Lockman Foundation | Scripture quotations marked BSB are from The Holy Bible, Berean Study Bible, BSB, Copyright ©2016, 2020 by Bible Hub Used by Permission. All Rights Reserved Worldwide. | Scripture quotations marked KJV are taken from the King James Version of the Bible. Public domain. | Scripture quotations marked MSG are taken from THE MESSAGE, copyright © 1993, 1994, 1995, 1996, 2000, 2001, 2002 by Eugene H. Peterson. Used by permission of NavPress. All rights reserved. Represented by Tyndale House Publishers, Inc. | Scripture quotations marked NKJV are taken from the New King James Version®. Copyright © 1982 by Thomas Nelson. Used by permission. All rights reserved. | Scripture quotations marked NLT are taken from the Holy Bible, New Living Translation, copyright © 1996, 2004, 2015 by Tyndale House Foundation. Used by permission of Tyndale House Publishers, Inc., Carol Stream, Illinois 60188. All rights reserved.

For foreign and subsidiary rights, contact the author.

Cover design by: Todd Petelle
Cover photo by: Andrew van Tilborgh

ISBN: 978-1-969062-07-0          1 2 3 4 5 6 7 8 9 10

Printed in the United States of America

FOREWORD BY DR. BENNY TATE

# THE SHIFT

## CREATING AN ENVIRONMENT FOR TRANSFORMATION

### JOHNNY H. MOORE

*This book is dedicated to my most prized possession,
my precious family—the ones who know me best,
yet love me most.*

*Dianne, my wife of thirty-seven years,
my best friend, my partner in life.*

*My sons and families:
Joshua and Hannah, Jude and Luke,
Jonathan and Ashley, Abigail and Emily.*

*My daughter and family,
Anna and John Thomas, Tripp.
You are all the greatest creative, visionary leaders I know.*

*I am beyond blessed to travel this journey with you!*

*I love you all!!
Dad*

# CONTENTS

*Foreword* . . . . . . . . . . . . . . . . . . . . . . . . . . . . . . . . . . . . . . . . xvii
*Acknowledgments* . . . . . . . . . . . . . . . . . . . . . . . . . . . . . . . . . . .xix
*Introduction* . . . . . . . . . . . . . . . . . . . . . . . . . . . . . . . . . . . . .21
CHAPTER 1. **THE DREAM** . . . . . . . . . . . . . . . . . . . . . . . . . . . . . . . . . . . . .31
CHAPTER 2. **S: SPIRITUAL LIFE** . . . . . . . . . . . . . . . . . . . . . . . . . . . . . . .45
CHAPTER 3. **H: HOSPITALITY** . . . . . . . . . . . . . . . . . . . . . . . . . . . . . . . . . 83
CHAPTER 4. **I: INTERDEPENDENCE** . . . . . . . . . . . . . . . . . . . . . . . . . .107
CHAPTER 5. **F: FOCUS OUT** . . . . . . . . . . . . . . . . . . . . . . . . . . . . . . . . . .131
CHAPTER 6. **T: TRANSFORMATION** . . . . . . . . . . . . . . . . . . . . . . . . . .161
CHAPTER 7. **CREATING A SHIFT** . . . . . . . . . . . . . . . . . . . . . . . . . . . . . .177
**CONCLUSION** . . . . . . . . . . . . . . . . . . . . . . . . . . . . . . . . . . . . . . .191

# FOREWORD

I truly believe that if a book has ever been written "for such a time as this," it is *The Shift*.

Johnny Moore, thank you! In America today, 85 percent of churches have either plateaued or are in decline. To say we need a shift is a great understatement.

This book isn't written from theory—it's born out of real-life experience and decades of faithful, proven leadership. I'm convinced that inspiration without information leads to frustration, and *The Shift* offers both. It provides the nuts and bolts for God to do a supernatural work of transformation in your life and in the life of your church or organization.

My hope is that every pastor, Christian leader, and parishioner in America reads this book. I only wish that, four decades ago, when I began in ministry, I could have read it. I truly believe I would be better for it—and so would my church.

## THE SHIFT

Congratulations to you for picking up this book. You're not just reading—you're stepping into a future where a great shift is possible.

—Dr. Benny Tate
Rock Springs Church
Milner, Georgia

# ACKNOWLEDGMENTS

Webster defines the word *choir* as "an organized group of persons or things." Writing a book is never a solo journey. It takes a choir. For me, I have been blessed to be surrounded by a choir of great people who, without them, this book would not exist.

My choir consists of:

My publisher, Martijn van Tilborgh, and the whole AVAIL team. All of you are amazing! God brought you all into my life to make dreams come true! Thank you for believing in me and partnering with me in this journey.

My church family at Family Worship Center. You have allowed me to be your pastor for over thirty-one years. Some of you have been with me since day one. Many of you have come along the way, have bought into this great mission and vision, and have been with me since you walked in the door. We have walked

# THE SHIFT

through good times and into difficult places together. You have stayed and served alongside me, and together, we have and are experiencing The SHIFT. Others came for a season and then left for greener pastures. However, for all of you who call Family Worship Center home—those in the building every week, and those who are part of our online family—your reward will be great!

To my incredible staff, Dianne Moore, Julie Barrineau, Nora Sutton, Joshua Moore, Jessica Schafer, and Jonathan Moore. You are the absolute best! Thank you for your unconditional love for me and your great sacrifice for this team and our church family. Having you in my life makes coming to work every day a great joy. I could never do what I do without you.

To my daughter, Anna—my personal editor of all my writing—you truly have a gift. Thank you for making me better than I really am.

And finally, and most importantly, I am thankful for the grace of the Lord Jesus Christ, the love of God, and the fellowship of the Holy Spirit. Without you, there would be no purpose, no mission, and no hope.

# INTRODUCTION

*INTRODUCTION*

Malcolm Gladwell opens his book, *The Tipping Point*, with this story:

*For Hush Puppies—the classic American brushed-suede shoes with the light crepe sole—the Tipping Point came somewhere between late 1994 and early 1995. The brand had been all but dead until that point. Sales were down to 30,000 pairs a year, mostly to backwoods outlets and small-town family stores. Wolverine, the company that makes Hush Puppies, was thinking of phasing out the shoes that made them famous.*

*But then something strange happened. At a fashion shoot, two Hush Puppies executives—Owen Baxter and Geoffrey Lewis—ran into a stylist from New York who told them that the classic Hush Puppies had suddenly become hip in the clubs and bars of downtown Manhattan. "We were being told," Baxter recalls, "that there were resale shops in the Village, in Soho, where the shoes were being sold. People were going to Mom-and-Pop stores, the little stores that still carried them, and buying them up."*

# THE SHIFT

*Baxter and Lewis were baffled at first. It made no sense to them that shoes that were so obviously out of fashion could make a comeback.*

*By the fall of 1995, things began to happen in a rush. First, the designer John Bartlett called. He wanted to use Hush Puppies in his spring collection. Then another Manhattan designer, Anna Sui, called, wanting shoes for her show as well. In Los Angeles, the designer Joel Fitzgerald put a 25-inch inflatable basset hound—the symbol of the Hush Puppies brand—on the roof of his Hollywood store. He gutted an adjoining art gallery to turn it into a Hush Puppies boutique. While he was still painting and putting up shelves, the actor Pee Wee Herman walked in and asked for a couple of pairs. "It was total word of mouth," Fitzgerald remembers.*

*In 1995, the company sold 430,000 pairs of the classic Hush Puppies. The next year, it sold four times that. The year after that, still more, until Hush Puppies were once again a staple of the wardrobe of the young American male. No one was trying to make Hush Puppies a trend. Yet, somehow, that's exactly what happened. The shoes passed a certain point in popularity, and they tipped. How does a $30 pair of shoes go from a handful of downtown Manhattan hipsters and designers to every mall in America in the space of two years?*[1]

---

1 Malcolm Gladwell, *The Tipping Point: How Little Things Can Make a Big Difference* (New York: Little, Brown, 2000).

Gladwell says that the *Tipping Point* was a result of three things:

1) Contagious behavior
2) Little changes that had big effects
3) Actions #1 and #2 both happened in a hurry

These three simple actions are what I call a "SHIFT!" If a simple SHIFT can cause a *Tipping Point* to occur for an outdated, out-of-style pair of shoes, there's no doubt that a divine SHIFT has the potential to cause a church, a business, or any organization to reach a *Tipping Point,* resulting in a transformation unlike anything it has ever experienced before.

## THE BOOK OF EZEKIEL

The Book of Ezekiel is a difficult book to understand. It has been said that the Jewish rabbis would not allow this book to be read to their young men until they were thirty years of age because they did not want them to look down on the Scriptures just because Ezekiel was so difficult to understand. Truthfully, however, it's easier to understand the book if you have a little knowledge of the history of Israel.

If you know anything about Israel, then you know that Israel had a bad habit of obeying God partially. Their worship struggled because of this habit, and their relationship with God became strained. God tells them that if they don't get these things worked out and commit to serving Him with their whole hearts, then their enemies will soon take them into captivity.

# THE SHIFT

Ezekiel comes on the scene when the Babylonians take Israel into captivity for the second time. Ezekiel prophesies during one of the most depressed and distressed times in Israel's history. When we get to chapter 37, Jerusalem has been destroyed. A refugee that survived the destruction comes to where Ezekiel is and begins to tell all the exiles that their city has been destroyed. Can you imagine how these people felt? Their greatest hope was to return to Jerusalem, and now that hope is gone. Totally destroyed! It would be like astronauts on a space shuttle finding out on their return trip that the earth had been destroyed—no place to go home to.

But, here's the good part: The night before this refugee arrives, Ezekiel begins to prophesy a message of hope. Listen to what he says:

> *The hand of the LORD was upon me, and He brought me out by the Spirit of the LORD and set me down in the middle of the valley; and it was full of bones. He caused me to pass among them round about, and behold, there were very many on the surface of the valley; and lo, they were very dry. He said to me, "Son of man, can these bones live?" And I answered, "O Lord God, You know." Again He said to me, "Prophesy over these bones and say to them, 'O dry bones, hear the word of the LORD.' Thus says the Lord GOD to these bones, 'Behold, I will cause breath to enter you that you may come to life. I will put sinews on you, make flesh grow back on you, cover you with skin and put*

breath in you that you may come alive; and you will know that I am the LORD.'"

So I prophesied as I was commanded; and as I prophesied, there was a noise, and behold, a rattling; and the bones came together, bone to its bone. And I looked, and behold, sinews were on them, and flesh grew and skin covered them; but there was no breath in them. Then He said to me, "Prophesy to the breath, prophesy, son of man, and say to the breath, 'Thus says the Lord GOD, "Come from the four winds, O breath, and breathe on these slain, that they come to life."'" So I prophesied as He commanded me, and the breath came into them, and they came to life and stood on their feet, an exceedingly great army.

Then He said to me, "Son of man, these bones are the whole house of Israel; behold, they say, 'Our bones are dried up and our hope has perished. We are completely cut off.' Therefore prophesy and say to them, 'Thus says the Lord GOD, "Behold, I will open your graves and cause you to come up out of your graves, My people; and I will bring you into the land of Israel. Then you will know that I am the LORD, when I have opened your graves and caused you to come up out of your graves, My people. I will put My Spirit within you and you will come to life, and I will place you on your own land. Then you will know that I, the LORD, have spoken and done it," declares the Lord.'"
—Ezekiel 37:1-14

# THE SHIFT

God says, through the prophet Ezekiel, that He is going to bring a SHIFT, and this SHIFT will not only cause these people to live again, but they will also experience a lift that would make anything they had experienced before seem small. God will stand them on their feet, and they will become *"an exceedingly great army,"* enabling them to fulfill God's purpose! I believe this is a picture of the New Testament church. Though statistics tell us that most churches in America are either plateaued or declining, I don't think we should settle for this—God doesn't want it for His church. He wants His church to be *"an exceedingly great army."* God said to the nation of Israel, "I will open your graves; I will bring you out; I will breathe My Spirit into you; You will come to life; I will place you in your own land." This is a divine SHIFT! Will you join me and believe God for a divine SHIFT of this proportion in the church today? If so, then keep reading— the SHIFT is on!

**Disclaimer**: Throughout this book, certain words within scripture passages have been bolded to highlight key concepts, emphasize thematic connections, and support the overall message of the text. These additions are intended to draw attention to important ideas and should not be viewed as alterations of the original scriptures.

# CHAPTER 1
# THE DREAM

*THE DREAM*

One Saturday morning several years ago, I woke up sometime around 6:00 a.m. As I lay in bed, I began thinking about a lot of things. I was thinking about our church, our congregation, and like any good pastor, I was thinking about things that some of our congregation were going through and about where God had brought us from and where we were that day. I mumbled a few words of prayer: "Lord, help our people; move in our church and bring those things You have promised us to pass." And then I dozed back off to sleep.

While I slept, I had a dream. It is just as real to me today as it was on the day I had it. We were in a Sunday morning church service. It was a large sanctuary, and people were scattered around in it. I know it was our sanctuary because I saw some of our people there. Praise and worship had just ended, and I was coming to the pulpit to preach. When I got there, something seemed odd. It felt like something was missing—like there was no congregation there. I felt an emptiness in my stomach. I felt alone. It felt like I was looking at a wall. Then, all of a sudden, it was like my eyes were opened—like a veil had fallen off my face. I suddenly realized that the stage was set up backwards. It was facing the same way the congregation was facing, and I was literally looking at the wall! I felt panic come all over me. In the dream, I cried out to the Lord and said, "Oh God, what is happening? What is

# THE SHIFT

going on here? What am I going to do?" Immediately, the Lord said, *"All you need is a shift."* I quickly spun around, and when I did, I saw that the sanctuary was now running over with people. People were everywhere, and others were still coming in the door, trying to find a place to sit. It was alive! It was full of people and full of the presence of God! It was unbelievable! At that moment, I woke up—wide awake! I got up, went into the living room, and sat down on the couch. Suddenly, I heard the Lord say:

> *"I am bringing a shift to My church. This shift will lift My church to a new place and a new level. It will open the door to a great harvest that has only been seen in your heart. You will soon see it with your eye. Prepare the people for the harvest that I am sending, for it is soon to come. Then you will know that I, the Lord, have spoken and done it,"* declares the Lord.

God is about to SHIFT gears in the church! Some people will embrace this SHIFT, while others will resist it. Some churches will embrace it, while others will hold to the patterns of the past. I am confident that this prophecy is for any church and any pastor who has a vision to reach their community. This is the heart of God! He cares about your town and your community, and He is looking for pastors and churches that will embrace His heart and do whatever it takes to reap the harvest in your town. If you want to be that church, then stop right now and say to the Lord, "I receive this prophecy for my life and my church. Bring it to pass in my life, in my church, in my town, Oh God!"

## GOD TAKES HIS TIME PUTTING THINGS IN ORDER, BUT WHEN HE GETS IT IN PLACE, HE MOVES IN A HURRY!

For many of us, God never moves fast enough. I'm not implying that He's ever late. But, there are just times when I wish He would move sooner! I'm reminded, even as I write today, of how God put a dream in my heart in the early '80s of having a church in my hometown that would impact our community and the surrounding region of Cairo, Georgia. I could see it! I could see myself standing in a large sanctuary preaching to hundreds— maybe thousands of people. I could see people running into the building to get saved, lives being changed, ministry flowing out of the building into the community and the surrounding areas. I could see people from all walks of life, every ethnic background, worshipping together and then leaving the building equipped and empowered to reach the harvest of this community and bring hope to our region. I thought it would happen in a matter of months. It didn't.

I remember driving out of Cairo seven years later in a U-Haul truck with tears running down my face, on my way to a God-ordained ministry assignment in Ocala, Florida. Questions flooded my mind: *Did I miss it? Was it just wishful thinking?*

## THE SHIFT

*Was it just a fantasy?* Nevertheless, I left. I buried the dream and went to another town, to serve another man, with another vision, at another church. I served him faithfully. I never looked back. Dianne and I worked hard. We gave everything we had to this man and his vision. God blessed our lives and our work, and only eternity will reveal the results of our time there and the fruit of our labor. While serving in this ministry assignment, God was working in ways I could not see. Jesus said:

> *"Truly, truly, I say to you, unless a grain of wheat falls into the earth and dies, it remains alone; but if it dies, it bears much fruit. He who loves his life loses it, and he who hates his life in this world will keep it to life eternal. If anyone serves Me, he must follow Me; and where I am, there My servant will be also; if anyone serves Me, the Father will honor him."* —John 12:24-26

Fast forward to July of 1994, packing the U-Haul once again. But this time, we were going home. My pastor and all the wonderful people at our church in Ocala, Florida, blessed us, anointed us, prayed for us, and sent us forth as missionaries to plant a brand new church in Cairo, Georgia. The dream would live again! It WAS God's dream. But, NOW was God's time. I thought it was gone, and I was content faithfully serving God in the place He had sent me. However, I have learned through the years that God knows what He's doing and He is always faithful! You see, God takes His time putting things in order, but when He gets it in place, He moves in a hurry!

## THE DREAM

Now, here I was on this Saturday morning, thirty-one years away from the first time I had this dream, and now, God said, *"Prepare the people for the harvest that I am sending, for it is soon to come."* It may seem to you that God is taking His time moving on your behalf. But I want to remind you to "let endurance have its perfect result, so that you may be perfect and complete, lacking in nothing" (James 1:4). Things may be moving slowly right now, but as you prepare yourself and your people, the SHIFT will happen, and when it does, it will happen quickly.

What is it going to take for your church to experience a transformation that will raise it to a renewed place of fruitfulness, effectiveness, and influence in your community? It's going to take a SHIFT. You may be asking, "So, what exactly is this SHIFT?" *Merriam-Webster* defines the word "shift" as meaning *"to change the place, position, or direction of."*[2] A SHIFT can be a powerful thing. One small SHIFT in the ocean floor can trigger a tsunami that could wipe out an entire nation. The 2004 Indian Ocean tsunami was among the deadliest natural disasters in human history, with over 230,000 people killed in fourteen countries bordering the Indian Ocean.[3] One SHIFT of a gear in a race car can unleash a whole new level of power and increased miles per hour. A SHIFT at the right time can be the difference between winning and losing the race. In the same way, when God initiates a divine SHIFT, it can lift a church to a whole new level of effectiveness. This SHIFT can transform and cause a congregation to

---
2  Merriam-Webster, s.v. "shift," https://www.merriam-webster.com/dictionary/shift#:~:text=a,make%20a%20change%20in%20(place).
3  Maila D. H. Rahiem et al., "Why did so many women die in the 2004 Aceh Tsunami? Child survivor accounts of the disaster," *ScienceDirect* 55 (2021), https://doi.org/10.1016/j.ijdrr.2021.102069.

come into its own, discover its purpose, and experience a new level of power. That church can then lock in to the daily journey of fulfilling its God-given mission.

The apostle Paul points out an interesting thought that gives even deeper insight into the SHIFT. Notice what he writes:

> *But God, being rich in mercy, because of His great love with which He loved us, even when we were dead in our transgressions, made us alive together with Christ (by grace you have been saved), and raised us up with Him, and seated us with Him in the heavenly places in Christ Jesus, so that in the ages to come He might show the surpassing riches of His grace in kindness toward us in Christ Jesus.* —Ephesians 2:4-7

Paul literally confirms what God says to Ezekiel. Though he uses different words, the message is the same:

- » "Son of man, can these bones live?" (Ezekiel) / "We were dead in our transgressions" (Paul)
- » "Behold, I will cause breath to enter you that you may come to life" (Ezekiel) / "made us alive together with Christ" (Paul)
- » "They came to life and stood on their feet" (Ezekiel) / "raised us up with Him" (Paul)
- » "An exceedingly great army" (Ezekiel) / "seated us with Him in the heavenly places in Christ Jesus" (Paul)

In reading and studying the writings of Paul, the Book of Ephesians has always been one of my favorites. I love preaching from this book and have developed my own mental picture of what happens when a person becomes a child of God from chapter 2. In my mind, I picture an unsaved person as one who is alive but not really living. I can see them lifeless—no purpose, no identity, no real passion—trying to make it in life all alone. But when they acknowledge and accept Jesus as Lord and Savior of their life, I see them coming alive with Christ. I see the blood of Jesus cleansing them from all sin, and I see God raising them up with Christ and seating them with Him in heavenly places. Wow! What a powerful scene!

---

## A GOD-ORDAINED SHIFT DOESN'T HAPPEN BY ACCIDENT. IT IS INTENTIONAL.

---

But over the past several months, that word "seated" has taken on new meaning. Read it again . . . "Even when we were dead in our transgressions, made us alive together with Christ (by grace you have been saved), and raised us up with Him, and **seated** us with Him in the heavenly places in Christ Jesus" (Ephesians 2:5-6). Seated does not mean "to just take a seat" or "to have a seat and rest awhile." No. It means to *"sit down; to set in place;*

# THE SHIFT

*to appoint; to settle in; to continue."*[4] The word "seat" means *to attach to or place firmly in or on something as a base.*[5] From this, I have modified my personal definition as, *"to be locked-in for the purpose of performing a task or assignment."* It is the picture of a chain locking into a sprocket; a gear locking Into position. Paul is implying, by the use of this word, that God has a fixed place for us; that He lifts us up and concretes us in! How would you like for your church to be "locked in" to God's plan? That is exactly God's intention. Again, Paul says that Christ has "seated us" with Him.

God has a place for each of us to be effective, and when He brings a divine SHIFT in our lives, a transformation occurs. He lifts us up and *seats* us in a new place. It's like shifting gears into overdrive. You move to a level that you have never entered before. It doesn't mean that all your problems go away. The roads are still bumpy and dangerous, no matter what kind of car you drive. But it does mean that you can now function at a level and at a pace that you've never functioned at before. You are locked in. You have found your groove. You have shifted gears. Ministry is meaningful. Ministry is profitable. You still deal with the enemy, but now, he's chasing you; you're not chasing him. He's trying to stop you; you're not trying to stop him. Instead of playing defense, your offense is now on the field. You are now able to score and win! You are seated in the place God intended you to be! You have experienced a divine SHIFT and have now

---

[4] *Bill Mounce Greek Dictionary*, paraphrase, s.v. "seated" *(kathizō)*, https://www.billmounce.com/greek-dictionary/kathizo.

[5] Dictionary.com, s.v. "seat," accessed October 7, 2025, https://www.dictionary.com/browse/seat.

been transformed into a powerful movement of God that the gates of hell cannot prevail against!

Think about it like this: When the Earth shifts, things fall, things crumble, things tumble to the ground. But when Heaven creates a shift, things lift, things grow, things rise. The interesting thing is that a God-ordained SHIFT doesn't happen by accident. It is intentional. God uses pastors, spiritual leaders, and businessmen and women to create an environment where a divine SHIFT can occur in the church, in your business, and in your life. In Ezekiel, it happened to an entire nation.

God has promised that He will bring a SHIFT to His church, and when churches experience it, they will be lifted to a whole new place of purpose and power. Towns and cities can be affected in a positive way by a church that has encountered a divine SHIFT. People, who in times past have appeared unreachable, are reached. Obstacles that have seemed like impossibilities become possible. The whole atmosphere of your church becomes contagious. It's the same thing that happened with the church in Acts 2 when three thousand people were saved. The church shifted and became an unstoppable force. It's time for a divine SHIFT to occur in the church once again. Can it happen? Of course, it can!

Before we get to the heart of this book, you need to pause for just a moment and ask yourself a few questions:

- » Do you believe it is God's will for your church to grow?
- » Do you want your church to grow?

# THE SHIFT

- » Do you believe that you could help your church grow?
- » Are you willing to do your part to help your church grow?

I hope you answered "Yes" to all these questions. If you did, then this book will give you some practical "How-to's" to create an environment that will result in a great move of God in your church. Take it in and immediately apply the principles I have laid out for you. The SHIFT is on!

Throughout this book, I will address the five areas that cause a SHIFT. I will write about each one using an acrostic based on the word S.H.I.F.T. While each of these areas is powerful on its own, none is sufficient to cause the SHIFT. All five have to work together in order for a divine SHIFT to occur. Are you ready? Well, let's get going . . .

# CHAPTER 2
# S: SPIRITUAL LIFE

## S: SPIRITUAL LIFE

I remember someone asking me as a kid, "Which comes first, the chicken or the egg?" Though I never really knew the answer to that question as a kid, there's no doubt that I know the answer now. The chicken came first. It all started with God, not an egg. God didn't create an egg. He created a chicken with the potential to lay an egg! We must understand that everything starts with God! Yes, that's right. It all starts with Him. All one has to do to discover this is to open the Bible to Genesis 1:1. It says, "In the beginning God. . . ." The New Testament confirms the same thing:

> *In the beginning was the Word, and the Word was with God, and the Word was God. He was in the beginning with God. All things came into being through Him, and apart from Him nothing came into being that has come into being. —John 1:1-3*

The SHIFT starts the same way—with God. God wants to bring a SHIFT to His church. It's His idea. He said it, and He will do it. Notice that it was God who spoke to Ezekiel and promised that the bones would live again. "Again He said to me, 'Prophesy over these bones and say to them, "O dry bones, hear the word of the LORD." Thus says the Lord GOD to these bones, 'Behold,

## THE SHIFT

I will cause breath to enter you that you may come to life'" (Ezekiel 37:4-5).

God said, "I will cause it to happen."

It was God who chose to create mankind, and it was God who put life into him. "Then the LORD God formed man of dust from the ground, and breathed into his nostrils the breath of life; and man became a living being" (Genesis 2:7). God later said to Moses, "You shall have no other gods before Me" (Exodus 20:3). When Jesus comes on the scene, He boldly declares, "YOU SHALL LOVE THE LORD YOUR GOD WITH ALL YOUR HEART, AND WITH ALL YOUR SOUL, AND WITH ALL YOUR MIND" (Matthew 22:37). In His famous Sermon on the Mount, Jesus issues the challenge to "Seek first His kingdom and His righteousness, and all these things will be added to you" (Matthew 6:33). John, the Revelator, points out that, though God is proud of our work and our accomplishments, these things will never take the place of relationship. God wants a relationship with His people more than anything else. John writes:

> *"I know your deeds and your toil and perseverance, and that you cannot tolerate evil men, and you put to the test those who call themselves apostles, and they are not, and you found them to be false; and you have perseverance and have endured for My name's sake, and have not grown weary. But I have this against you, that you have left your first love."* —Revelation 2:2-4

## S: SPIRITUAL LIFE

The Word is telling us again what we should already know—"everything starts with God." To experience a divine SHIFT in our personal lives, in our churches, and in our businesses, we must begin with our spiritual lives. The SHIFT always starts here. Here are four steps to a healthy spiritual life.

## STEP 1: SPIRITUAL DISCIPLINES

If the divine SHIFT begins with the spiritual life of people and the congregation, then it is a given that spiritual disciplines are a must. There can be no compromise here. Spiritual disciplines must become a way of life for us. Every pastor and leader must build their lives around spiritual disciplines. As a spiritual leader, not only should we model these disciplines, but we should also teach them to those we lead. To position our church for a SHIFT, we are responsible for raising the spiritual climate in our congregation.

My long-time friend and mentor, Dr. Wayne Lee, says in his book *The Church Life Model* that "Healthy congregations have a balanced, vital, and dynamic spiritual life that gives thrust to the church's mission. Relationship with God, knowing and experiencing Him, certainly serves as the central human motivation of the Christian life and also for participation in the church." It is impossible to experience this on a consistent basis without a commitment to spiritual disciplines. Dr. Lee continues by pointing out that "congregations that promote spiritual life observances and activities experience bursts of spiritual life and release a continuous flow of spiritual reality within the church." Your spiritual life gives power, thrust, and life to everything you do.

# THE SHIFT

Authors such as Dallas Willard,[6] Richard Foster,[7] and Gil Stieglitz[8] have written exceptional works that can assist believers in understanding and practicing spiritual disciplines. However, in this work, I only want to focus on three. Dr. Wayne Lee, with over forty years of research and study of the local church as a university vice president, professor, and veteran pastor of three megachurches, has concluded that while all of the spiritual disciplines are vital and necessary, these three have the potential to bring a lift to any church—devotions, prayer, and worship.[9]

## DEVOTIONS

This discipline is too often underrated and minimized in the life of a believer. Its power is overlooked and underestimated. If it were possible to put all that we do as pastors and leaders into a pot and boil it down to one ingredient, much of what we do would evaporate. I believe that the ingredient that would remain—that has the power to determine our effectiveness more than anything else—would be our devotion life. If you do not have a consistent devotion life, all that remains in your pot is steam—hot air! The quality of a person's spiritual life can always be traced back to their private devotions. We have to live this and teach this to our congregations. Based upon what I have discovered in our congregation, I believe that if 40 percent of any congregation would spend fifteen to thirty minutes in

---

6   Dallas Willard, *The Spirit of Disciplines: Understanding How God Changes Lives* (San Francisco, CA: HarperOne, 1999).
7   Richard Foster, *Celebration of Discipline: The Path to Spiritual Growth* (San Francisco, CA: HarperOne, 2018).
8   Gil Stieglitz, *Spiritual Disciplines of a C.H.R.I.S.T.I.A.N.: Intensive Training in Christian Spirituality* (Principles to Live by, 2011).
9   Wayne Lee and Sherry Lee, *The Church Life Model: A Biblical Pattern for the Spirit-Filled Church* (Lake Mary, FL: Creation House, 2011).

private devotions, five out of seven days a week, the outward results would be astounding.

---

> ## IF YOU REQUIRE THEM TO GROW, THEN YOU WILL DISCOVER THAT THEY WILL.

---

Every pastor and congregational leader must model and apply this spiritual discipline. Several years ago, in my personal time of prayer and devotion, I asked the Lord how I could better disciple and develop my leaders. He impressed upon me to teach them how to have devotions. I learned that most people do not know how to have a devotion—even those who have been in church all their lives. We tell people to "read the Bible and pray," but sadly, most do not know how to do this. They may not tell you, but they are asking themselves things like, *Where do I start reading? How much do I read? What do I pray about? How long do I pray?* They need a plan, and so I decided that I would share what I do and give them a daily plan to follow. Here are three simple action steps to assist you with devotions:

**1) Develop a personal growth plan for your congregation.**
Most Christians want to have regular devotions and grow in their faith, but most really do not know how. They need the proper tools to assist them and guide them on that journey. As a pastor,

it is my responsibility to help my congregation grow, and I do that by preparing and providing a 365-day personal growth plan. This plan is designed to help them grow in four specific areas: intellectual growth, physical growth, spiritual growth, and social growth. Luke 2:52 tells us that "Jesus kept increasing in wisdom and stature, and in favor with God and men." If it was important for Jesus to grow in these areas, then it is important for us too. To request a sample copy of our personal growth plan, scan the QR code.

**2) Require a one-year commitment from your leaders to participate in this growth plan.**
If you require nothing from your leaders, then that is exactly what you will get in return—nothing. Real leaders step up to the plate. If you require them to grow, then you will discover that they will. However, it is important that you put resources in their hand to help them grow. Thus, the purpose of the growth plan. I have found that leaders are looking for a challenge, and when I require them to participate in a yearly growth plan with me, they rise to the top and take the bait. I've also found that if I don't challenge them, they will gravitate towards other compelling interests. Another exciting part is that when I mention something in my Sunday message that we've read or prayed about from our daily devotions, it helps me connect with them more deeply.

**3) Hold each other accountable.**
Accountability is a healthy thing. We all need it. The best leaders want it. One reason great leaders became great is that they

were held accountable. Truthfully, real leaders long for pastors to hold them accountable, and in return, our leaders hold us accountable too. Accountability is a mutual thing. The proverb writer said, "Iron sharpens iron, So one man sharpens another" (Proverbs 27:17). We keep each other sharp when we hold each other accountable.

**PRAYER**

I know this sounds trite, but the spiritual discipline of prayer must be practiced privately and publicly. Every pastor knows the importance and the power of prayer. We have all spent hours in prayer for our churches and our people. However, raising up others in your congregation to pray for the church with you is one of the most rewarding parts of prayer. This is one of the greatest ways to get your congregation to buy in to your leadership and vision. Research shows that it takes ten hours of prayer a week per one hundred people to lift a church[10]

Think about this. The average church size in America hovers around eighty to ninety people, depending on which pollster you follow. If you were to calculate the amount of time spent in prayer specifically for a church of this size, you would discover that the pastor and the pastor's wife spend about eight to ten hours a week in prayer combined for the church. Therefore, the church runs approximately eighty to one hundred in attendance on Sunday. What would happen if you were to enlist ten more people to commit to praying one hour a week each, specifically for your church? The amount of time spent weekly

---

10  Wayne H. Lee, *Church Consultation Manual* (Church Life Resources, LLC, 2012).

# THE SHIFT

in prayer for the church would jump from eight to ten hours to possibly twenty hours.

Here's the point: If a church averages one hundred people on Sunday and you want to grow the church to two hundred, it will require increasing the amount of passionate prayer specifically for that church. To move to two hundred, the church needs twenty people to commit to praying passionately for the church at least one hour per week. I know somebody's thinking right now that all I'm doing is reducing prayer to a means for church growth. That is not my goal, but the truth remains: Your church needs the prayer, and you need the practice! So, just do it and see what happens! Here are a few action steps that will energize your church's prayer life:

**1) Establish a purpose-driven prayer ministry.**
One of the most neglected ministries in churches is usually the prayer ministry. It's easy to take the people praying for your church for granted. As pastors, we generally encourage the congregation to pray for their church, and we assume that they do. Think about it like this: If we want to minister to the children of our church, we start a children's ministry. We do the same for every other need in the church. We appoint a leader, we form a team, we train volunteers, and then we do ministry together.

Here's a thought: Why do we do this for every area except prayer? Every church must begin a purpose-driven prayer ministry. In other words, we need to find a leader who is passionate about prayer. We need to build a team and train our volunteers. Then we need to give them "prayer assignments" that target specific areas in the church, such as areas of need, areas of concern, areas of battle, areas of mission and vision. Truthfully, if everything we attempted in the natural passed first through the passionate prayer of the prayer ministry, we would experience far greater results and success in the things we set our hands to do.

**2) Include prayer in every ministry.**
Every ministry in the church needs specific, targeted prayer. While it is important that the prayer ministry pray specifically for the church's ministries, it is just as important that those involved in individual ministries also pray for *their* ministry. In other words, every volunteer involved in children's ministry should be praying for the children's ministry. The same goes for every other ministry in the church. No one knows what you need and what you deal with in those ministries better than you. You are in the heat of the battle week after week. You are the "boots on the ground." You see the needs. You feel the pain of those you minister to. You see the struggle of those you minister with. You and your team are the ones who are most passionate about that ministry. You and your team are anointed to pray and intercede for the ministry in which you serve. James tells us that passionate people pray powerful and effective prayers. "The earnest (heartfelt, continued) prayer of a righteous man makes tremendous power available [dynamic in its working]" (James 5:16, AMPC).

## THE SHIFT

**3) Schedule specific times for congregational prayer for the church.**

Every church should periodically schedule a time for a prayer meeting. Many churches struggle to find times for the congregation to come together for corporate prayer. The calendar is already stressed with all the different functions and activities of the church, and sadly, prayer usually becomes the caboose. Our church has battled the calendar issue, trying to find dates and times for prayer, and truthfully, sometimes the calendar wins. But we have learned that we must schedule these times and put them on the calendar first, then all the other activities can be scheduled around these dates. We try to schedule a time of corporate prayer at least quarterly.

Here are some things that have worked for us: Every year in January, beginning on the first Sunday of the year, we begin our 21 Days of Prayer and Fasting. We encourage the entire church to join us. I create a "5-Point Prayer Card" that gives us a road map for our prayer focus, and we distribute this card to everybody in the church. We also make it available electronically for those who would prefer to use their phone or tablet. During the fall, we schedule a twenty-four-hour prayer chain. We select twenty-four prayer captains and ask them to sign up for one of the twenty-four hours of the prayer chain. We ask them to recruit a team of others who will meet them at the church during their designated hour to pray. Generally, it starts at 8:00 on Saturday morning and ends at 8:00 on Sunday morning. We also schedule a couple of Wednesday nights throughout the year to have what we call a "refresh service." We ask all our classes to meet in the sanctuary for a night of worship and prayer.

Most recently, I preached a series on prayer titled "A Call to Prayer." At the end of the series, I shared that I wanted to enlist one hundred people to become "Pastor's Prayer Partners." I asked them to commit to praying for me and the church ten minutes a day, Monday through Friday, if they signed on. I discouraged them from signing up if they were not going to do it. At the time of this writing, I have 106 people committed to this ministry. I usually send them a text once a week with a thank you and a prayer focus for the week. Already, we have seen incredible results from their prayers.

---

**ATTENDANCE AT A WEEKEND WORSHIP SERVICE WILL DEMONSTRATE WHETHER WORSHIP IS A PRIORITY IN THE CHURCH YOU CALL HOME.**

---

**WORSHIP**

The spiritual discipline of worship must become a priority for a church to experience a divine SHIFT. People need to become aware, once again, of the importance of attending church

# THE SHIFT

regularly. New Christians should be taught that attending church regularly and consistently is vital to their spiritual health. Dr. Lee writes that "Healthy congregations have dynamic worship services in which most of the active members participate."[11]

Every congregant should be challenged to commit to attending at least one worship service a week 90 percent of the time—that equals forty-seven out of fifty-two weeks. The bottom line is that you just need to come to church! Everybody needs to be in their place: ushers, greeters, choir/praise team and band, elders, teachers, and everybody else. People will always have to attend to emergencies, vacations, and other events that arise, but as the pastor, you should continue to remind the people to be in church every opportunity that they can. Our culture today requires us to do things differently, which means that we should use every available resource we have to remind our people to be in church. Attendance at a weekend worship service will demonstrate whether worship is a priority in the church you call home. The church should also provide a worship service that is beneficial to those attending. Here are some suggestions that have proven helpful for us in creating a worship service that people can't resist:

**1) Provide a dynamic and structured worship service.**
Pastors, you have to have a plan for your morning worship service. You can't just shoot from the hip anymore. You can no longer blame your lack of planning on, "We just want the Spirit to move!" Plan the service. Create a service outline. Put it in

---
[11] Lee and Lee, *The Church Life Model*.

## S: SPIRITUAL LIFE

the hands of everybody involved in the service. Don't waste the people's time. Ask yourself, *What do I want to accomplish in this service today?* Take what you see in your Spirit and flesh it out. God is a God of order, so plan the "order" of the service. Paul said, "But all things must be done properly and in an orderly manner" (1 Corinthians 14:40).

**2) Strive for excellence in every area.**
You must give your best in every service. After all, if it's a worship service, then you should offer the best service you have as worship to God. This means to put the best people you have up front. Let the best singers sing. Let the best musicians play. Preach the best sermon you've ever preached. Let the best person receive the offering. Let the best person make announcements. Let the best person do Scripture and prayer. Quit having a "cattle-call" choir. If they aren't willing to give extra time to rehearse and practice, then cut it out altogether. However you structure your service, make sure you give God and your people your best.

Listen, one more thing . . . it has to be done this way every week! You can't just do this on special days—every Sunday is a special day! One of our most-attended services every year is what we call "back-to-school Sunday." A few years ago, one of our school principals attended this service for the first time. After the service, she came and asked me, "Do you all have service like this every week?" I said, "Yes, ma'am, every Sunday is just as special as this one." She and her whole family came back the next week, and they have been a vital part of our church now for several years.

# THE SHIFT

**3) Preach a series that provides guidance and direction.**
Many pastors preach sermons every week, and they aren't sure what they are going to preach next week until it gets closer to Sunday. I know this because I used to operate this way. Our church changed when I began preaching series. I have discovered that when I announce on Sunday that I am beginning a four-week series next Sunday and give them the title of the series, people arrange their schedules to come back because they don't want to miss the series. We will talk about this in another chapter in more detail, but I learned that you have to take people on a "preaching journey." If you offer them an invitation to join you for a four-week series, you'll be amazed at how many will take you up on it. You must preach for results, and you must offer them simple ways to apply what you preach. I promise, preaching in series will make you a better preacher!

**4) Follow up on people who are absent.**
In order to offer our best worship to God, we must find ways to follow up on new people who attend, as well as those who haven't been in two or three weeks. These people matter to God, and they should matter to us. God obviously sent us guests because He thought we would take good care of them. We will discuss systems for follow-up in another chapter, but we must understand that the way we follow up on our guests and keep up with our people is a major part of our worship. If we take care of the guests that come, then God will send us more. If we don't follow up on them, then God will send them somewhere else.

## STEP 2: SPIRITUAL PEOPLE

The second step to a healthy spiritual life is to become a true spiritual people. I believe the number one responsibility of a pastor is to make disciples. One of my all-time favorite books is Bill Hull's *The Disciple-Making Pastor*.[12] Every pastor should become a student of this book. We spend way too much time doing everything except the one thing that we have been called to do—make disciples. Making disciples is extremely hard work and takes a large amount of time. I guess this may be one reason so many pastors choose not to do it. Some pastors would rather preach and shout and tell others what they should be doing. They would rather visit hospitals all day and eat lunch with the senior citizens and listen to them talk about what a wonderful pastor they are and how much they really need them. While there is nothing wrong with these things, we cannot spend all our time doing them at the expense of making disciples. Making disciples is about investing our lives in others. It's about teaching and training people to "do the work of ministry" (Ephesians 4:12, author paraphrase). Making disciples is about helping people grow in their faith and become real "spiritual people."

---

12  Bill Hull, *The Disciple-Making Pastor: Leading Others on the Journey of Faith* (Ada, MI: Baker Books, 2007).

# THE SHIFT

---

## GOING TO CHURCH DOESN'T MAKE A PERSON SPIRITUAL ANY MORE THAN GETTING IN THE WATER MAKES SOMEONE A FISH.

---

What people say does not determine spirituality. What they do does. The apostle Paul, in his letter to the church at Galatia, writes:

> *But the fruit of the Spirit is love, joy, peace, patience, kindness, goodness, faithfulness, gentleness, self-control; against such things there is no law. Now those who belong to Christ Jesus have crucified the flesh with its passions and desires. If we live by the Spirit, let us also walk by the Spirit.* —*Galatians 5:22-25*

Paul is reminding us that our walk speaks louder than our talk. Many people live under the assumption that if they go to church, they are spiritual. Going to church doesn't make a person spiritual any more than getting in the water makes someone a fish. Don't get me wrong—spiritual people go to church. But many people have been to church all their lives and still are not spiritual. Being religious and being spiritual are not necessarily the same thing. Many church people have grown old but have never grown up.

In his first letter to the church at Corinth, Paul addresses this same issue with them. Notice what he says:

> And I, brethren, could not speak to you as to spiritual men, but as to men of flesh, as to infants in Christ. I gave you milk to drink, not solid food; for you were not yet able to receive it. Indeed, even now you are not yet able, for you are still fleshly. For since there is jealousy and strife among you, are you not fleshly, and are you not walking like mere men? For when one says, "I am of Paul," and another, "I am of Apollos," are you not mere men? —1 Corinthians 3:1-4

Paul points out that spiritual immaturity is a problem that must be addressed. He says, "I wanted to talk to you as spiritual people, but you were not ready." He's not implying that they are unsaved because he addresses them as "brethren." He just recognizes that they are spiritually immature—"infants," he calls them. They could be referred to as "carnal Christians." They were Christians who had never been discipled. Paul implies that spiritual maturity will cause one to live on a higher level. In verses 3 and 4, Paul uses a phrase that has always intrigued me. He says, "Are you not walking like mere men?" What does that mean—"mere men"? It means that "you are walking like an ordinary man without God—living in selfishness, pride, and envy."

# THE SHIFT

Spiritual people are recognized by certain characteristics. Here are just a few:

**1) Spiritual people display expressions of compassion.**
Just look at Jesus. On several occasions, the writers of the Gospels testify that Jesus was "moved with compassion" (Matthew 9:36; Matthew 14:14; Matthew 20:34; Mark 1:41; Mark 6:34; Luke 7:13). One of the greatest stories of spirituality in the Bible is the story of the Good Samaritan. Notice what happened:

> *But a Samaritan, who was on a journey came upon him; and when he saw him, he felt compassion, and came to him and bandaged up his wounds, pouring oil and wine on them; and he put him on his own animal, and brought him to an inn and took care of him.* —Luke 10:33-34

Just like Jesus, the Good Samaritan's compassion moved him. Jesus ends this story with these words: "Go and do the same" (Luke 10:37).

**2) Spiritual people give and receive forgiveness.**
Once again, we witness this lived out in the life of Jesus. Some of His final words while He was on the cross were: "Father, forgive them; for they do not know what they are doing" (Luke 23:34). Jesus also taught His disciples the importance of forgiveness: "Then Peter came and said to Him, 'Lord, how often shall my brother sin against me and I forgive him? Up to seven times?' Jesus said to him, 'I do not say to you, up to seven

times, but up to seventy times seven'" (Matthew 18:21-22). The connection between giving and receiving was one of the most important aspects of forgiveness that Jesus taught His disciples when He said: "And forgive us our debts, **as we** also have forgiven our debtors. . . . For if you forgive others for their transgressions, your heavenly Father will also forgive you. But if you do not forgive others, then your Father will not forgive your transgressions" (Matthew 6:12, 14-15). There is nothing easy about this. Growing up in the Lord and developing spiritual maturity are tough!

**3) Spiritual people are disciples.**
Just knowing a lot about God doesn't make anyone spiritual. Spiritual people are those who actually follow Jesus—not like "roadies" following the newest pop star, but like learners trying to become like the one they are following. The New Testament calls these people *disciples.* When Jesus chose His disciples, He promised that if they would follow Him, He would make something out of their lives (Matthew 4:19). Jesus instructed them to practice what He taught them—to live it out in their everyday lives—and pointed out that "My Father is glorified by this, that you bear much fruit, and *so* prove to be My disciples" (John 15:8). In His final words to His disciples, He challenged them to do for others what He had done for them—make something out of their lives. This challenge should also become our mission:

> *"Go therefore and make disciples of all the nations, baptizing them in the name of the Father and the Son and the Holy Spirit, teaching them to observe all that*

> I commanded you; and lo, I am with you always, even to the end of the age." —Matthew 28:19-20

The key here is this—you must be a disciple in order to make one!

## STEP 3: SPIRITUAL GIFTS

The third step of a healthy spiritual life is understanding spiritual gifts. God Himself has given gifts to every one of His children. There are no exceptions. Many are of the assumption that only those who stand behind the pulpit have spiritual gifts. While it is true that those individuals possess specific gifts given by God, it is also true that every believer sitting in the congregation has God-given gifts as well. The apostle Paul, in his letter to the church at Ephesus, acknowledges five different offices that are filled by people with corresponding gifts, namely, the apostle, the prophet, the evangelist, and the pastor-teacher. However, if you read on through the rest of the chapter, it's easy to see that there is a specific role that all those in the congregation fill based upon the gifts they have been given. Let's take a look:

> And He gave some as apostles, and some as prophets, and some as evangelists, and some as pastors and teachers, for the equipping of the saints for the work of service, to the building up of the body of Christ; until we all attain to the unity of the faith, and of the knowledge of the Son of God, to a mature man, to the measure of the stature which belongs to the fullness of Christ. As a result, we are no longer to be children,

*tossed here and there by waves and carried about by every wind of doctrine, by the trickery of men, by craftiness in deceitful scheming; but speaking the truth in love, we are to grow up in all aspects into Him who is the head, even Christ, from whom the whole body, being fitted and held together by what every joint supplies, according to the proper working of each individual part, causes the growth of the body for the building up of itself in love.* —Ephesians 4:11-16

Paul is instructing those with the aforementioned gifts to equip, train, and deploy the rest of the body of Christ into ministry in the church. As we noted earlier, this is the process called *discipleship*. He goes on to say that this is how the body of Christ is built. He points out that there is a specific role that each individual part is to play, and then he adds, "according to the proper working of each individual part." The implication is that everyone who is a part of the body of Christ has a part to play if the church is going to grow into maturity. That *part* is determined by the gift, or gifts, that God has given each believer. Take a look at this same scripture in *The Message*:

*But that doesn't mean you should all look and speak and act the same. Out of the generosity of Christ, each of us is given his own gift. The text for this is,*
  *He climbed the high mountain,*
  *He captured the enemy and seized the plunder,*
  *He handed it all out in gifts to the people.*

# THE SHIFT

> *Is it not true that the One who climbed up also climbed down, down to the valley of earth? And the One who climbed down is the One who climbed back up, up to highest heaven. He handed out gifts above and below, filled heaven with his gifts, filled earth with his gifts. He handed out gifts of apostle, prophet, evangelist, and pastor-teacher to train Christ's followers in skilled servant work, working within Christ's body, the church, until we're all moving rhythmically and easily with each other, efficient and graceful in response to God's Son, fully mature adults, fully developed within and without, fully alive like Christ.*
>
> *No prolonged infancies among us, please. We'll not tolerate babes in the woods, small children who are easy prey for predators. God wants us to grow up, to know the whole truth and tell it in love—like Christ in everything. We take our lead from Christ, who is the source of everything we do. He keeps us in step with each other. His very breath and blood flow through us, nourishing us so that we will grow up healthy in God, robust in love.* —Ephesians 4:7-16 (MSG)

It is really mind-boggling how many Christians know nothing about spiritual gifts. If you are Pentecostal, then of course you've heard about the gift of tongues and interpretation. But, sadly, many Pentecostals know very little about any of the other gifts. If you are of another denominational persuasion, then you may have been taught to shy away from spiritual gifts, or even that spiritual gifts have passed away.

Nothing could be further from the truth! God has given the church spiritual gifts to enable us to complete this last-day ministry of the church.

Let me take a minute and give you some biblical facts about spiritual gifts:

**1) Spiritual gifts are needed for a happy body.**
For a physical body to be healthy and function correctly, all parts must be in working order. If an arm is broken, it will affect the overall performance of the body. If a foot decides that it's tired of being walked on, it'll take the week off; then, the whole body suffers. It's the same in a spiritual body—the body of Christ. When people decide, *I'm not going to show up today*, it affects the performance of the entire body, regardless of how insignificant that individual may think they are. Again, the apostle Paul addresses this issue with the church at Corinth:

> *For the body is not one member, but many. If the foot says, "Because I am not a hand, I am not a part of the body," it is not for this reason any the less a part of the body. And if the ear says, "Because I am not an eye, I am not a part of the body," it is not for this reason any the less a part of the body. If the whole body were an eye, where would the hearing be? If the whole were hearing, where would the sense of smell be? But now God has placed the members, each one of them, in the body, just as He desired. If they were all one member, where would the body be? But now there are many*

*members, but one body. And the eye cannot say to the hand, "I have no need of you"; or again the head to the feet, "I have no need of you."* —1 Corinthians 12:14-21

It's like putting a jigsaw puzzle together. Which piece is not important? All of them are important, no matter how big or small they are, and the puzzle is not complete if any piece is missing. This is what Paul was implying when he wrote: "From whom the whole body, being fitted and held together by what **every** joint supplies, according to the proper working of **each individual part**, causes the growth of the body for the building up of itself in love" (Ephesians 4:16). There is nothing more frustrating than having almost finished a puzzle only to realize that four pieces are missing! For a church to be healthy and effective, every believer should use their spiritual gifts.

**2) Every believer has been given at least one spiritual gift.**
Most Christians have been given more than one spiritual gift, but it is a fact that every believer has been given at least one. Peter tells us that each one has been given a gift. "As **each one** has received a *special* gift, employ it in serving one another as good stewards of the manifold grace of God" (1 Peter 4:10). Paul echoes the same message. "But to **each one** of us grace was given according to the measure of Christ's gift. Therefore it says, 'WHEN HE ASCENDED ON HIGH, HE LED CAPTIVE A HOST OF CAPTIVES, AND HE GAVE GIFTS TO MEN'" (Ephesians 4:7-8).

Again . . . "Since we have gifts that differ according to the grace given to us, **each of us** is to exercise them accordingly: if prophecy, according to the proportion of his faith" (Romans 12:6).

And again . . .

> Now concerning spiritual **gifts**, brethren, I do not want you to be unaware. . . . Now there are varieties of gifts, but the same Spirit. And there are varieties of ministries, and the same Lord. There are varieties of effects, but the same God who works all things **in all persons**. But to **each one** is given the manifestation of the Spirit for the common good.
> —1 Corinthians 12:1, 4-7

Just in case you are wondering, let me say it again: If you are a born-again Christian, you have been given at least one spiritual gift!

### 3) Each believer is most effective when working in their area of giftedness.

Many times, Christians are guilty of working outside of their areas of giftedness. As pastors and leaders, this is sometimes necessary simply because when things need to be done, they need to be done—and the lot falls on us if there is nobody available to do it. However, our responsibility as pastors is to help people discover their gifts and give them the opportunity to use them. The Word is very clear that different people have different gifts, and it is also clear that people find their greatest

## THE SHIFT

joy and effectiveness when they serve in the area of giftedness. Notice Paul's exhortation in his letter to the Romans:

> For through the grace given to me I say to everyone among you not to think more highly of himself than he ought to think; but to think so as to have sound judgment, as God has allotted to each a measure of faith. For just as we have many members in one body and all the members do not have the same function, so we, who are many, are one body in Christ, and individually members one of another. Since we have gifts that differ according to the grace given to us, **each of us is to exercise them accordingly:** if prophecy, according to the proportion of his faith; if service, in his serving; or he who teaches, in his teaching; or he who exhorts, in his exhortation; he who gives, with liberality; he who leads, with diligence; he who shows mercy, with cheerfulness.
>
> Let love be without hypocrisy. Abhor what is evil; cling to what is good. Be devoted to one another in brotherly love; give preference to one another in honor; not lagging behind in diligence, fervent in spirit, serving the Lord; rejoicing in hope, persevering in tribulation, devoted to prayer, contributing to the needs of the saints, practicing hospitality. —Romans 12:3-13

*The Message* offers a down-to-earth paraphrase. Take a look at verses 4-8:

## S: SPIRITUAL LIFE

*In this way we are like the various parts of a human body. Each part gets its meaning from the body as a whole, not the other way around. The body we're talking about is Christ's body of chosen people. Each of us finds our meaning and function as a part of his body. But as a chopped-off finger or cut-off toe we wouldn't amount to much, would we? So since we find ourselves fashioned into all these excellently formed and marvelously functioning parts in Christ's body, let's just go ahead and be what we were made to be, without enviously or pridefully comparing ourselves with each other, or trying to be something we aren't.*

*If you preach, just preach God's Message, nothing else; if you help, just help, don't take over; if you teach, stick to your teaching; if you give encouraging guidance, be careful that you don't get bossy; if you're put in charge, don't manipulate; if you're called to give aid to people in distress, keep your eyes open and be quick to respond; if you work with the disadvantaged, don't let yourself get irritated with them or depressed by them. Keep a smile on your face.*
—Romans 12:4-8 (MSG)

Paul says, "Whatever your gift is, you need to use it to the best of your ability!" (author paraphrase)

Many times, people try to be something they were never gifted to be. They think because they want to sing, that they are gifted

## THE SHIFT

to sing—when everybody listening knows this is not the case. Some may want to teach, but they may not be gifted to do so. Others may be gifted to lead but would rather sit back and let someone else do it. Nevertheless, the truth remains that you will find your greatest joy, your greatest effectiveness, and your greatest reward working and serving in the areas where you are gifted. You will also benefit the church and the kingdom of God in greater ways by serving in the area where God has gifted you.

**4) Every believer is responsible to discover, develop, and deploy their spiritual gifts.**
If every believer knew what their gifts were, worked diligently to develop them, and served in a ministry where they could best use their gift, the church would move to a new level almost overnight. Sometimes gifts are discovered while you are in deployment. I am not a fan of waiting until you discover your gift before you get involved. You might not discover your gift until you *are* involved. The key is to get connected, get involved in a ministry, and as you are serving, you very well could discover what your gift is. Once you discover your gift, you are then responsible for developing it.

---

## THERE ARE TOO MANY GIFTED CHRISTIANS SITTING ON THE PEW DOING NOTHING WITH THE GIFTS GOD GAVE THEM.

---

Paul exhorts us to make this process a priority:

> *Until I come, give attention to the public reading of Scripture, to exhortation and teaching. Do not neglect the spiritual gift within you, which was bestowed on you through prophetic utterance with the laying on of hands by the presbytery. Take pains with these things; be absorbed in them, so that your progress will be evident to all.* —1 Timothy 4:13-15

Most churches have a handful of people who do all the work and ministry in the church, meaning that they have too many spectators and not enough participants. Every Christian should be connected to and involved in the ministry of a local church. One of the primary ways to do this is to commit yourself to an area of ministry in that local church by using the spiritual gift or gifts that God has deposited in your life. Peter affirms this thought by saying, "As each one has received a *special* gift, employ it in serving one another as good stewards of the manifold grace of God" (1 Peter 4:10).

Once you discover your gift, get plugged in to an area of ministry where you can develop that gift. It's impossible to develop anything that is dormant. Your gift must be deployed; it must be put into action. There are too many gifted Christians sitting on the pew doing nothing with the gifts God gave them. It's really a scary place to be. Why? Because every Christian will one day stand before God and give an account of what they did with the gifts God gave them. I seriously doubt that our excuses for not being engaged in ministry will be good enough when we stand before God. The apostle Paul understood the seriousness of this responsibility when he said, "For the gifts and the calling of God are irrevocable" (Romans 11:29).

At Family Worship Center (FWC), we encourage the use of spiritual gifts. We value them. We need them, and we provide opportunities to use them. Many of you reading this today want to do something great! If you are a Christian, then God has equipped you to do something great! You must not be afraid to begin using the gifts that you possess. Again, the apostle Paul admonishes us to "kindle afresh the gift of God which is in you through the laying on of my hands. For God has not given us a spirit of timidity, but of power and love and discipline" (2 Timothy 1:6-7). Even if you are not a Christian, God has gifts wrapped with your name on the tag. He's waiting on you to receive Him so He can deposit them into your life. Quit putting it off. Quit trying to achieve greatness alone. Shift into a new gear and begin today to experience a new level of living.

## STEP 4: SPIRITUAL THINGS

The fourth step to a healthy spiritual life is that of spiritual things. Spiritual things are a by-product of the first three steps. "Spiritual disciplines produce spiritual people who use spiritual gifts to do spiritual things." God has some spiritual things on His agenda that He wants you and me to do. You see, a spiritual life is made up of all of these things working together to accomplish something bigger than any of these parts individually.

When spiritual disciplines become the end in themselves, the result is always legalism. If being spiritual people was the only goal for our lives, we would never be able to connect with others around us. If spiritual gifts were the measuring stick for spirituality, then we would all be puffed up with pride and arrogance. A spiritual life is about all these things working together to accomplish the purpose and plan of God. As I said before: "Spiritual disciplines produce spiritual people who use spiritual gifts to do spiritual things."

In John 14, we see Jesus preparing His disciples for His departure. They are unsure about His words and are trying, in their limited way of thinking, to process all that Jesus is laying on them. As I read the first few verses, I can picture the disciples scratching their heads, looking at each other, and wondering, *What in the world is He talking about?* Take a look:

> *"Do not let your heart be troubled; believe in God, believe also in Me. In My Father's house are many dwelling places; if it were not so, I would have told you; for I go to prepare a place for you. If I go and prepare a place for you, I will come again and receive you to Myself, that where I am, there you may be also. And you know the way where I am going." Thomas said to Him, "Lord, we do not know where You are going, how do we know the way?" Jesus said to him, "I am the way, and the truth, and the life; no one comes to the Father but through Me." —John 14:1-6*

# THE SHIFT

Thomas had some questions, and so did Philip. After answering Thomas, Jesus answers Philip's question with a question:

> *Jesus said to him, "Have I been so long with you, and yet you have not come to know Me, Philip? He who has seen Me has seen the Father; how can you say, 'Show us the Father'? Do you not believe that I am in the Father, and the Father is in Me? The words that I say to you I do not speak on My own initiative, but the Father abiding in Me does His works. Believe Me that I am in the Father and the Father is in Me; otherwise believe because of the works themselves." —John 14:9-11*

Jesus says, "Philip, if you have listened to My words, and watched My life, it shouldn't be hard for you to tell that I have come from God" (author paraphrase). Then He drops the big one on him: "If you can't wrap your faith around my words, then just believe because of the things I have done" (author paraphrase). Again, "Spiritual disciplines produce spiritual people who use spiritual gifts to do spiritual things." This is exactly what the disciples saw when they looked at Jesus. But hold on a minute! Jesus didn't stop there. He looked at all of them and said, "Truly, truly, I say to you, he who believes in Me, the works that I do, he will do also; and greater *works* than these he will do; because I go to the Father" (John 14:12). He said, "greater things"—spiritual things! One more time, I repeat, "Spiritual disciplines produce spiritual people who use spiritual gifts to do spiritual things." Here are three simple places where "spiritual things" should show up:

## 1) In our walk

Spiritual things should show up in our everyday walk. Most of the miracles and signs in the New Testament took place outside of the temple. While spiritual things should certainly take place in our churches today, we should not limit the work of God to a building we call the church. God expects spiritual things to occur in our everyday walk as Christians. Acts 10:38 gives us a picture of what our everyday walk should look like: "*You know of* Jesus of Nazareth, how God anointed Him with the Holy Spirit and with power, and *how* He went about doing good and healing all who were oppressed by the devil, for God was with Him." All of us should be walking in the anointing God gave us, doing good and healing all those who are oppressed by the devil. Our walk should be overflowing with spiritual things!

## 2) In our witness

As Christians, God has called us to be witnesses. Our testimony should be the same as the apostle Paul's when he said, "For I am not ashamed of the gospel, for it is the power of God for salvation to everyone who believes" (Romans 1:16). When we share the Word of God, we can expect the power of God to be present. Spiritual things happen when we include God's Word in our witness. Jeremiah 1:12 (author addition) says that God is "watching over [His] Word to perform it." Psalm 103:20 says that the angels perform the Word of God and obey the voice of the Word of God. Therefore, every time we use the Word of God in our witnessing, angels are dispatched to bring the Word that we share to pass. When we witness with the Word of God, spiritual things will happen!

## THE SHIFT

**3) In our work**
Every one of us is called to do the work of God. Jesus said, "Greater things than these shall you do" (John 14:12, author paraphrase). We should pray for people any time an opportunity arises: in the mall, on the job, at the beauty shop, at the gym, at the post office, at the ballpark, in the restaurant, and every other place we go. Jesus said, "These signs will follow those who believe" (Mark 16:17, NKJV). If we are doing the work of God, we should expect spiritual things to occur.

The SHIFT always starts with our spiritual lives. There is simply no other place to start. Call your church to prayer. Preach a series on how to have an effective devotion. Challenge your people to be in church every week. Begin teaching on spiritual gifts on Wednesday nights. Become a disciple-making pastor.

Pastor, you must begin raising the spiritual climate of your church. When you do, you will begin creating an environment for transformation. This is where it all starts. This is the foundation for a SHIFT. But this is only the beginning. Once you have begun to implement the spiritual life disciplines, it's time to move into the second phase of the journey—a subject that is rarely talked about, but one that plays a major role in the SHIFT.

# CHAPTER 3
# H: HOSPITALITY

## H: HOSPITALITY

I don't think I have ever heard a sermon on this subject. Truthfully, I'm not sure I've ever heard any teaching on it, except growing up in the Moore house. Growing up, my home was always warm and welcoming. People loved to come to our house. I remember families gathering at our house after church on Sunday nights for coffee and fellowship. Nobody wanted to go home. The kids would run and play outside, while the adults laughed and talked around the dining room table.

My mom was, even at ninety-one years old when she passed, a classy lady. She knew how to make everyone feel at home. When folks came to our house, they lacked for nothing. She waited on everyone, cooked for everyone, loved on everyone, and was genuinely glad they were there. My dad, who passed away at eighty-seven years of age, kept the conversation going around the table. I always loved hearing him laugh. He would keep everybody laughing and feeling right at home.

The amazing thing about my home growing up was that all my friends loved to come to our house. They felt loved, accepted, and welcomed. Most of my friends called my parents "Mom and Dad" because that's how they treated them. We never locked our doors, and my friends would come and go like they were at their house. It was nothing for them to walk in, go to the kitchen, and start looking around for something to eat. If my mom saw them, she would ask, "Do you want me to cook you some eggs and bacon?" And, more times than not, they would say, "That would be great, Mom!" I've watched my parents practice "hospitality" all of my life. They loved people, cared for them, ministered to them, prayed for them, laughed with them, cried with them, held them in their arms, and let Jesus strengthen them. I have witnessed my parents model in our home what should be modeled in the church.

In the process of the SHIFT, hospitality is right next to spiritual life. Though some may think this subject is light and shallow, and even unimportant, I believe it is vital to creating an environment for a SHIFT because hospitality is a reflection of a church's spiritual life. If the spiritual life of a church is vibrant, it will show up in how the church treats people—those within and those without.

Not enough attention is given to this subject. We train people how to preach, how to teach, how to lead, how to pray, and so on, but we never train our people how to be hospitable. I have discovered in pastoring the same church for over thirty years that this topic could be the difference maker in your life and your church.

Believe it or not, "hospitality" is a Bible word. There are numerous places in the Word of God where the word "hospitality" is implied, encouraged, and expected. There are five places where the word is actually used:

Romans 12:10-13:
> *"Be devoted to one another in brotherly love; give preference to one another in honor; not lagging behind in diligence, fervent in spirit, serving the Lord; rejoicing in hope, persevering in tribulation, devoted to prayer, contributing to the needs of the saints, practicing **hospitality**."*

1 Peter 4:7-9:
> *"The end of all things is near; therefore, be of sound judgment and sober spirit for the purpose of prayer. Above all, keep fervent in your love for one another, because love covers a multitude of sins. Be **hospitable** to one another without complaint."*

Hebrews 13:1-2
> *"Let love of the brethren continue. Do not neglect to show **hospitality** to strangers, for by this some have entertained angels without knowing it."*

1 Timothy 3:2
> *"An overseer, then, must be above reproach, the husband of one wife, temperate, prudent, respectable, **hospitable**, able to teach."*

Titus 1:7-8
> *"For the overseer must be above reproach as God's steward, not self-willed, not quick-tempered, not addicted to wine, not pugnacious, not fond of sordid*

## THE SHIFT

*gain, but **hospitable**, loving what is good, sensible, just, devout, self-controlled."*

You question the importance of "hospitality"? Just look where the word is found—in the same sentences as love, prayer, diligence, discipline, and leadership. There is no question about how important prayer and leadership are; however, hospitality is just as important in the life of a Christian and the life of a church.

Let's take a minute to define the word:

1) **Hospitality:** The friendly reception and treatment of strangers and guests; the quality or disposition of receiving and treating guests and strangers in a warm, friendly, and generous way.[13]
2) The Greek form of this word is *philoxenia*, which means to entertain strangers; to treat like a friend; to act fond; to be friendly.[14]

Personally, I believe hospitality starts with the pastor and his spouse. I hate to say it, but pastors are some of the most unfriendly people I have ever met. They can get so locked into their own little world that they forget that God sent us to reach people, and reaching people starts with loving people, caring for people, smiling at people, waving at people, speaking to

---
13 Women of the ELCA, "Hospitality: More than warm and friendly," 2009, https://www.womenoftheelca.org/filebin/pdf/resources/Hospitality.pdf.
14 Strong's Greek Lexicon, paraphrase, s.v. "hospitality" *(philoxenia)*, https://biblehub.com/greek/5381.htm.

people, talking to people, and taking time with people. My wife, Dianne, knows not to send me to Walmart if she's in a hurry for something. For me, just a quick trip to Walmart to get a loaf of bread can take an hour! I can't help it! Walmart is full of people, and I have to walk slowly among them. You never know who you might see or what they might need. Churches generally take on the personality of their pastor, so if I want my church to show true hospitality, then it must start with me.

Why are churches not hospitable? If you ask most church members if their church is friendly and hospitable, they will tell you quickly, "Yes, by all means, we are the friendliest church in town!" I have discovered that most churches are hospitable to those they know and see every week. But, to find out if your church is friendly, you must ask the first-time guests who attend your church, not the regular attenders.

---

**THE REALITY IS, IF YOU WILL BE A BLESSING, GOD WILL SEE TO IT THAT YOU ALWAYS RECEIVE ONE.**

---

I have discovered four reasons most churches are not hospitable:

# THE SHIFT

**1) They are ingrown.**
We walk into church, hug those we know, hang out with those we like, say hello to those we've already seen, and hide from those we don't know. We act like the church is our little club. We think everything should be done the way we like it. We're ingrown. We think, *This is my seat, This is my parking spot.* Some people mark their spot by leaving their Bible in their seat all week or their blanket to say, "No trespassing!" We look at people we don't know, like, *Who is that?* or *What are they doing here?* When our middle son, Jonathan, was in college, he got up one Sunday and went to find him a church to attend. He walked into a church, and the service had just started. When he walked in, all seventy of the attendees turned around and stared at him. He smiled and found him a seat. During the "meet and greet" time, he stood there while everybody greeted everybody, but him. When the service was over, he slowly made his way to the door, thinking somebody would eventually say, "Hello, it was good to have you today." But not one person spoke to him the entire time. He said, "Dad, I felt like the invisible man!" These people knew nothing about hospitality. They, like so many others, were only interested in themselves and their little group. They are ingrown.

**2) They are more interested in "getting" a blessing than they are in "being" a blessing.**
In most churches, everybody is focused on receiving for themselves. Truthfully, everybody comes to God because we are in need. We need a Savior. We need peace. We need purpose. We have problems, and many times our problems drive us to God.

But there comes a time in our spiritual growth and development that we should realize that we need to be a blessing, rather than always coming to church to get one. The reality is, if you will be a blessing, God will see to it that you always receive one. We must choose to be a blessing, be hospitable, show that you care about others, reach out to others, and give of yourself to others. God will always take care of you!

### 3) They see ministry as "a job to do" rather than "a service to provide."

Many people are involved in ministry at FWC on Sunday mornings. It is exciting and rewarding for our church to see so many people actively involved in ministry. We should all be responsible in ministry like we would be on a job—be on time, be dependable, and do your job. But, if we're not careful, we can get so focused on "doing our ministry" that it *becomes* a job. We can easily forget that we are in ministry to provide a service, not just do a job. When we're "just doing a job," we can become critical, judgmental, frustrated, cantankerous, and even bitter. There is nothing hospitable about any of this. Our job is people. Make no mistake about it, there is no ministry without people. We are here to serve people, and serving people is what hospitality is all about.

### 4) They are burdened down with their own problems.

Too many times, churches cease to be hospitable because everybody becomes so focused on their own problems that they are in no shape to care for other people. They can't smile. They can't be friendly. They can't pray for others. All they see are their own

## THE SHIFT

situations and problems. Again, the Word of God tells us, "Therefore humble yourselves under the mighty hand of God, that He may exalt you at the proper time, casting all your anxiety on Him, because He cares for you" (1 Peter 5:6-7). It also says, "I can do all things through Him who strengthens me" (Philippians 4:13). As pastors and leaders, we all have legitimate problems of our own. But we must learn to trust God to minister to us and meet our needs while we are caring for and being hospitable to others. When we grow to a place where we can push our own needs to the side in order to love, to care for, and minister to others, it is then that true hospitality can begin to flow from our lives. This is the true test of spiritual maturity. If you can be hospitable to others while you, yourself, are in need, then a SHIFT is about to happen in your life!

One of my favorite stories in the Bible is found in 1 Samuel 22. It is the story of David when he was on the run from King Saul, who was out to kill him. David was hiding from Saul in the Cave of Adullam. When his family learned where he was, they came to him, and the scripture says, "Everyone who was in distress, and everyone who was in debt, and everyone who was discontented gathered to him; and he became captain over them. Now there were about four hundred men with him" (1 Samuel 22:2). Think about this. Here is David running for his life. He's hungry, thirsty, tired, weary, and has his own problems to worry about. Then, all of a sudden, four hundred people show up at his door, not to help him, but expecting him to help them! They are in distress, in debt, discontented—just a bunch of needy people! But notice what he did. He took them in, showed them hospitality, promised to be their captain, and poured his life into them. He helped them. He took care of them. He trained them. He was hospitable to them even when he himself was in need. The exciting part is that these needy people eventually became known as "David's Mighty Men!"

Jesus was our greatest example. He loved and cared for people everywhere He went. I want our church to be known as the friendliest, most loving and caring church in this whole region! I want our church to be a church that truly loves people! All people. Good people. Bad people. Tall people. Short people. Skinny people. Blessed people. Red people. Yellow people. Black people. White people. All people!

The question is, "How can we do this?" How can our church show true hospitality to the people that come to us—the good people, the healthy people, and the people who are in distress, in debt, and discontented?

How about you? How about your church? What will it take for your church to be more hospitable? Here are three things that have worked for us:

**1) See every Sunday as a special day.**
Hospitality starts by seeing beyond yourself. Every pastor should wake up every Sunday expecting it to be a big day! You should walk out the door looking for God to show up! Every service at your church should be viewed as a special day. Whatever you do to connect with people on big days, you should do every

## THE SHIFT

Sunday. Think about this—what do you do on Easter? You plan the service. You know exactly what's going to happen, who is going to do it, and when it is going to be done. You probably write up a service outline. You make sure you have greeters in place, ushers in place, and cards and gifts prepared for first-time guests. We have valets in the parking lot to help park cars, welcome new people, assist those who need assistance, and bring people to the front door on a golf cart. Here's my point: If you do this on Easter, then why don't you do it every Sunday? The Sunday after Easter is just as important to God as Easter. The reason most churches don't do this is that it takes work. It takes planning. It takes preparation. But actions like these spell "hospitality" to those who pull in your parking lot and walk in your front door. It says, "We were expecting you to come, and we are glad you are here!"

---

# THE ONLY THING YOU CAN TAKE WITH YOU TO HEAVEN IS PEOPLE.

---

At FWC, we plan four "special services" every year. They are: Easter, Back-to-School Sunday, I Love This Church Sunday (Friend Day), and Christmas. The only thing that is different about these four services from every other Sunday is the advertising, but other than that, we see every Sunday as a special day. We treat our guests as special at every service. The Sunday after these special days is just as exciting as the special day because we plan it that way. We plan every service. We refuse to "wing it" or "shoot from the hip." We have a service outline prepared for every service, and everyone who is involved in the service has a copy of the service outline. If you want to be hospitable, then it must be planned. Whatever we do to connect with people on special days, we should do every Sunday! The psalmist David said:

> *This is the LORD's doing;*
> *It is marvelous in our eyes.*
> *This is the day which the LORD has made;*
> *Let us rejoice and be glad in it. —Psalms 118:23-24*

A little later, he said, "I was glad when they said to me, 'Let us go to the house of the LORD'" (Psalms 122:1). Notice what happened in the early church after the day of Pentecost:

> *So then, those who had received his word were baptized; and that day there were added about three thousand souls. They were continually devoting themselves to the apostles' teaching and to fellowship, to the breaking of bread and to prayer.*
>
> *Everyone kept feeling a sense of awe; and many wonders and signs were taking place through the apostles. . . .*
>
> *Day by day continuing with one mind in the temple, and breaking bread from house to house, they were taking their meals together with gladness and sincerity*

# THE SHIFT

*of heart, praising God and having favor with all the people. And the Lord was adding to their number day by day those who were being saved.*
—*Acts 2:41-43; 46-47*

This is what happens when we prepare and expect every Sunday to be a special day.

**2) Treat every person as a special person.**
People are God's most prized possession. People are who Jesus died for. The only thing you can take with you to heaven is people. If people matter to God, they should matter to us. Therefore, every person who comes to your church is special. As pastors, we must understand that God is holding us accountable for how we treat those He sends us. If we take care of the guests who come, they will keep coming. If we do not take care of them, the flow of new people will stop.

Most people are quick to respond to those they know and those who can do something for them. But what about those you don't know? What about those who can't do anything for you? What about the drug addict, the biracial family, the couple that lives together with three kids yet are not married, and the gay or lesbian couple? How do we treat these people? To be hospitable means that we treat all of them like Jesus would treat them. We love them, we embrace them, we value them, and we make them feel special.

## H: HOSPITALITY

I have had pastors say to me from time to time, "You know, people just aren't my thing—I focus my attention on preaching!" If that's how you think, then I would say to you what I said to them—"Fake it, then!" I don't care how good a preacher you are; without people, you have no one to preach to! You had better fall in love with people and begin to see them all as special! But, until you can do that from your heart, just fake it and do it because Jesus said to. I have learned that if I don't treat all people special, then neither will my congregation. If I do it, so will they. Let's take the advice of the wise man: "A man that hath friends must shew himself friendly: and there is a friend that sticketh closer than a brother" (Proverbs 18:24, KJV).

Jesus said, "For God so loved the world, that He gave His only begotten Son, that whoever believes in Him shall not perish, but have eternal life. For God did not send the Son into the world to judge the world, but that the world might be saved through Him" (John 3:16-17). Hospitable people are people who love the "whosoever"s, and hospitable churches are churches that also love the "whosoever"s. The Hebrew writer reminds us to, "Let love of the brethren continue. Do not neglect to show hospitality to strangers, for by this some have entertained angels without knowing it" (Hebrews 13:1-2).

Jesus reminds us:

> "For I was hungry, and you gave Me something to eat; I was thirsty, and you gave Me something to drink; I was a stranger, and you invited Me in; naked, and you

*clothed Me; I was sick, and you visited Me; I was in prison, and you came to Me." Then the righteous will answer Him, "Lord, when did we see You hungry, and feed You, or thirsty, and give You something to drink? And when did we see You a stranger, and invite You in, or naked, and clothe You? When did we see You sick, or in prison, and come to You?" The King will answer and say to them, "Truly I say to you, to the extent that you did it to one of these brothers of Mine, even the least of them, you did it to Me." —Matthew 25:35-40*

How would we respond if Jesus came knocking on our door wanting something to eat? We would treat Him as special! We must treat every person who comes through our doors as if they were Jesus. Jesus said, "When you feed them, you feed Me." He said, "When you help them, when you love them, it was really Me you helped and loved!" This is biblical hospitality.

**3) Use every situation as an opportunity to glorify God.**
Every situation people face is unique and should be handled by compassionate people who have been trained to deal with special situations. When a church is prepared to deal with unique situations, be it medical emergencies, security issues, safety issues, or any other situation that may arise, true hospitality is displayed. Most God-given opportunities don't come wrapped in foil paper and a red bow. Most of them arrive wrapped in difficulty, trouble, interruptions, and even sometimes pain.

I remember one specific situation that arose during a Sunday morning service at our church. Our praise team was leading in worship, and a lady in the choir passed out and fell to the ground. Now, in most Pentecostal churches, she would have died because the congregation would have assumed that she fell out in the Spirit! Our security team, which has medical personnel, immediately responded while another team member called 911. They checked her vitals and discovered that her blood pressure had dropped. They got her secured, and when the EMTs arrived, they ushered them in, loaded her on the stretcher, rolled her out, and transported her to our local hospital. (This is another example of people flowing in their gifts). Praise and worship never stopped. Of course, we prayed for her, but our security team handled the situation with grace and professionalism. They showed hospitality to her, and the entire congregation was amazed at how smoothly the entire situation was handled. It gave them, and our guests, comfort knowing that our church was prepared to handle special situations.

Every church will face difficult situations at some point. Being hospitable is about glorifying God in all those situations. It is our responsibility as pastors to train people and have them in place, ready to handle situations like these and others. The apostle Paul exhorts us by saying, "Whatever you do in word or deed, do all in the name of the Lord Jesus, giving thanks through Him to God the Father" (Colossians 3:17). In his letter to the church at Ephesus, he says, "With good will render service, as to the Lord, and not to men, knowing that whatever good thing each one does, this he will receive back from the Lord, whether slave or free" (Ephesians 6:7-8).

He also reminds us:

> *Now He who supplies seed to the sower and bread for food will supply and multiply your seed for sowing and increase the harvest of your righteousness; you will be enriched in everything for all liberality, which through us is producing thanksgiving to God. For the ministry of this service is not only fully supplying the needs of the saints, but is also overflowing through many thanksgivings to God. Because of the proof given by this ministry, they will glorify God for your obedience to your confession of the gospel of Christ and for the liberality of your contribution to them and to all"*
> —*2 Corinthians 9: 10-13*

Again, our greatest example, Jesus Himself, was hospitable to each of us. He was the Good Samaritan who found us half-dead lying by the side of the road. He came to us, brought healing to our lives, and promised to care for us. This story is the most relevant story in the Bible that shows hospitality in action.

If we are going to be a church where biblical hospitality flows naturally, we must first live it ourselves. Secondly, we must build this into the DNA of our congregation. We do that when we intentionally preach it, teach it, and train our people to do it. Let's face it, pastor, your people really do not know how to do this. When we began our greeter ministry, we trained our entire team through role play. Our team leaders set up a training session where they literally acted out the proper way for a team member to act. They showed them how greeting should be done and how it should not be done. It was amazing to watch these leaders at work, and it proved to be a turning point for our greeter ministry. We have also done the same type of training for our usher ministry.

Here are a few simple steps we have used that you could implement to make hospitality a priority:

**1) Develop systems to track first, second, and third-time guests.** When new people come to your church for the first time, they are obviously searching for something. Sadly, many churches are not prepared for first-time guests. Therefore, their follow-up is weak, and most of the time, the first timers do not return. This is why systems are so important. For a guest to return the second time, a connection has to be made the first time they come. Through the years, we have used many different ways to locate and register our guests, but none have worked as effectively as our connection card. Every week in our bulletin, we have a QR code that takes them to a connection card. We also display it on the screen for those who don't have a bulletin. I mention the connection card and the QR code every Sunday from the pulpit, but the most important player in the equation is the greeter. If the greeters are paying attention, they can facilitate getting the connection card filled out better than anyone because it is a person-to-person contact. After service, we gather the connection cards, enter the data, and send them a personal text message when service is over, thanking them for coming to FWC that day.

On Mondays, our staff process the cards and send our first-time guests a personal email from me. These things are almost a guarantee that our first-time guests will return the second time. When they return the second time, they receive a handwritten note from me, thanking them for coming, and with the note, we include a coupon for a free beverage from our *HomeBrood Cafe*.

**2) Create assimilation teams to integrate people into the church.** The days of new people just walking into your church and automatically getting involved are gone. Like it or not, if you leave people to themselves, they will leave. We teach our congregation that everyone is a greeter and everyone is an usher. We use the old business adage, "Everyone is in the sales department!" It doesn't matter what area of ministry people serve in; everyone is always on the lookout for guests. Several of our Sunday teams also serve as assimilation teams, including our valets, greeters, ushers, altar team, and our children's registration team. These are the front-line teams, and they are always working to make contact with those coming in the parking lot, the front door, the sanctuary doors, and the children's drop-off area. Don't ever leave people standing alone in the foyer trying to figure out where to go. If you do, chances are high that they won't return.

**3) Continue recruiting, enlisting, and training team members.** New people want to feel like they are needed. We are firm believers that the sooner we can get people connected to a ministry team, the more likely they are to stay. At FWC, we have many different ministry teams, and there are different requirements for involvement on each team. Some ministries, like children's and youth ministries, require that the individual have a criminal background check to get involved. However, our hospitality teams are perfect places for new people to get involved rather quickly. A few weeks ago, Dr. Lamar Vest, former General Overseer of the Church of God and former president/CEO of the American Bible Society, said to me, "For years, the church has expected people to believe before they were allowed to belong. But, I have discovered that what people need is a place to belong before they really believe." This has proven true for us at FWC. After people have attended for a few weeks, we reach out to them to get them connected to a team. Once they are connected to a team and feel that FWC is a place where they belong, they will immediately and officially join the church.

Every team leader understands the importance of building their team, so they have an eye for recruitment. Not all people will stay on the same team forever. They might want to eventually get involved in another area of ministry, so every leader must always be reaching for and training new people. John Maxwell calls it "The Law of the Bench."[15] Every ministry needs to have a strong bench so that if someone wants to move into another

---

15 John Maxwell, *The 17 Indisputable Laws of Teamwork: Embrace Them and Empower Your Team* (Nashville, TN: HarperCollins Leadership, 2013).

area of ministry, there is always someone trained and standing in the wings ready to step into their place.

**4) Regularly evaluate, expand, and improve the process.**
No system is perfect. There are always changes that must be made along the way. However, you have to start somewhere. The purpose of the system is to achieve the desired results. The system is not sacred. The results are. If the system you have in place is not producing the desired results, you have to keep adjusting it until it does—or else get a new system. It's like the headlights on your car. The purpose of the lights is not just to burn. The purpose of the lights is to provide light on the road in front of you to give direction for the journey, and to help you get to where you're going. Sometimes, they have to be adjusted.

---

# YOU DON'T WORK FOR THE SYSTEM. THE SYSTEM HAS TO WORK FOR YOU.

---

I got in my wife's Jeep a few nights ago and realized as I was driving to town that her headlights were shining directly down on the road, making it hard to see ten feet in front of us. It almost drove me crazy. So, the next day, I took it to the Jeep dealer and had them adjust the lights. They tightened up the adjustment screws, which raised the headlights. That night, when I got in

## H: HOSPITALITY

the Jeep to drive it home, it was like driving a new vehicle. Our systems are the same way. You have to look at each of them, and if they are not producing the results that you want, you have to tighten or loosen the screws until they produce. If they still don't produce, then you might have to replace them. You don't work for the system. The system has to work for you.

Hospitality is so important in the process of a SHIFT. Our churches must be the most friendly and welcoming places in town. It should be like pulling into the parking lot at Disney World. There should be people smiling, waving, giving direction, and providing service everywhere you turn. Our churches must be a place where people want to come. When we create an exciting, warm, and hospitable environment, people will start lining up to get in.

# CHAPTER 4
# I: INTERDEPENDENCE

## I: INTERDEPENDENCE

God would have never given us the Great Commission to go into all the world and preach the gospel if He never intended for that to really happen. However, no pastor can fulfill this calling by himself, no matter how gifted he may be. God is holding all of us accountable to fulfill the mission He has given us. But we have to understand that none of us can do it alone. God never intended for us to do it alone—but we can do it together.

Peter has always been one of my favorite disciples. He seemed to be a "get it done" kind of person, even to a fault. I believe that he really loved Jesus and wanted to represent Him well, but he also appeared to be a very impatient and immature person. When something needed to be done, he was probably the first one to raise his hand. He was not afraid to make decisions and was not one to wait on other people. Like many of us, I think his motto would have been, "If you won't help me, I'll just do it myself."

Therefore, his tendency was to take matters into his own hands, which got him into trouble with Jesus many times. One thing that I really like about Peter, though, was that he was teachable. When Jesus corrected him, he did his best to change. As a matter of fact, when you follow his life throughout the gospels, you can easily see that Jesus was grooming him for something great.

# THE SHIFT

When Jesus looked at Peter, He saw the day of Pentecost. Jesus knew he had the potential to do something big. The "Peter" that we see coming out of the Upper Room was not the "Simon Barjona" that we see leaving his boat and following Jesus.

When we read 1 and 2 Peter, it's almost hard to believe that the author was the same guy who said, "Woman, I do not know Him" (Luke 22:57). One thing I do notice in Peter's writings, however, is that he addresses some of his own insecurities and immaturities that haunted him in his earlier years. It's obvious that he had come to understand what interdependence was all about. He was no longer a "lone ranger." He knew what Jesus had sent him to do, but he had matured to the place where he understood the importance of patience, forgiveness, compassion, and timing. But he also knew that he could not fulfill God's call alone. It is out of his own experience that he writes, "The Lord is not slow about His promise, as some count slowness, but is patient toward you, not wishing for any to perish but for all to come to repentance" (2 Peter 3:9).

The Holy Spirit would not have inspired Peter to write this if it were not possible. But, like Peter, we, too, must come to the realization that we cannot do this alone. We have to work together towards a common goal, with everybody pulling together and rowing in the same direction. At FWC, our mission defines our common goal.

*I: INTERDEPENDENCE*

> **THE FWC MISSION:**
> *"Family Worship Center is a community of Spirit-Filled believers committed to God's purpose of changing lives, by worshipping God, leading others to Jesus, and building unified teams to care for all in every stage of life."*

This is our mission, and we believe God is holding us accountable to fulfill this God-given mission. Our mission requires that we do ministry with interdependence at the core.

Pastor Wayne Cordeiro, in his book *Doing Church as a Team*, says:

> *May we learn God's design for His people and begin to respect and appreciate each other's giftings. There are few things more beautiful to God than seeing His people serving and working together in a unified rhythm. It's like a symphony to His ears. That's how we were created to function. God has designed us to need each other! For us to reach our communities, much less the world, we will need every ministry doing its part and every member of the congregation excitedly doing church as a team.*[16]

This is "interdependence." Interdependence is defined as *"a relationship in which each member is mutually dependent*

---

[16] Wayne Cordeiro, *Doing Church as a Team: The Miracle of Teamwork and How It Transforms Churches* (Raleigh, NC: Regal Books, 2001), 20.

# THE SHIFT

*on the others."*[17] The apostle Paul believed that the church was designed to be interdependent. In his writings, he gives us a picture of interdependence though he does not specifically use the word:

Romans 12:4-5:
> "For just as we have many members in one body and all the members do not have the same function, so we, who are many, are one body in Christ, and **individually members one of another**."

1 Corinthians 12:14-21:
> "For **the body is not one member, but many**. If the foot says, 'Because I am not a hand, I am not a part of the body,' it is not for this reason any the less a part of the body. And if the ear says, 'Because I am not an eye, I am not a part of the body,' it is not for this reason any the less a part of the body. If the whole body were an eye, where would the hearing be? If the whole were hearing, where would the sense of smell be? But now God has placed the members, each one of them, in the body, just as He desired. If they were all one member, where would the body be? But now **there are many members, but one body**. And the eye cannot say to the hand, 'I have no need of you'; or again the head to the feet, 'I have no need of you.'"

---

17 Definitions, s.v. "interdependence," https://www.definitions.net/definition/interdependence.

Verses 25-26:
> "So that there may be no division in the body, but that the members may have the same care for one another. And **if one member suffers, all the members suffer with it; if one member is honored, all the members rejoice with it.**"

Ephesians 4:16:
> "From whom the whole body, **being fitted and held together by what every joint supplies, according to the proper working of each individual part**, causes the growth of the body for the building up of itself in love."

This is "interdependence." Interdependence is not the same as independence. Independence is defined as *"freedom from the control, influence, support, aid, or the like of others."*[18] This sounds good at face value, but the truth is that one day you look around and discover that you are all alone. You don't have any support, any help, or anyone around you to lift you up, to encourage you, or to work with you, and it's then that you realize just how small and inadequate you really are. God never intended for any of us to be this way. Satan resisted interdependence and operated in an independent spirit. He rebelled against God and fell. An independent spirit is a weakness, not a strength.

---
18  Dictionary.com, s.v. "independence," https://www.dictionary.com/browse/independence.

# THE SHIFT

## WE MUST BECOME INTERDEPENDENT IF WE'RE GOING TO BE SUCCESSFUL IN FULFILLING OUR MISSION.

Stephen Covey, in his classic book *The Seven Habits of Highly Effective People,* makes the following observation:

> *Independent thinking alone is not suited to interdependent reality. Independent people who do not have the maturity to think and act interdependently may be good individual producers, but they won't be good leaders or team players. They're not coming from the paradigm of interdependence necessary to succeed in marriage, family, or organizational reality.*[19]

I have discovered that if you are going to experience the SHIFT in your personal life, your church, or your business, and enter into the place of fruitfulness and effectiveness that God has for you, then you are going to have to rid yourself of that independent spirit. This *I don't need anybody; I can make it on my own; It's going to be my way or the highway* type of thinking has got to go.

---

[19] Stephen Covey, *The Seven Habits of Highly Effective People: Powerful Lessons in Personal Change* (New York, NY: Free Press, 1989), 59.

## I: INTERDEPENDENCE

We must become interdependent if we're going to be successful in fulfilling our mission. Our conversation must be inclusive when we're referring to ministry. We need to understand that I need you. You need me. We need each other. You have what I don't have. I have what you don't have. Together, we have everything we need to fulfill God's mission in this town, in this region, and in the world! There are no limits to what we can accomplish for God if we understand and embrace interdependence. There are four steps to embracing interdependence.

## STEP 1: SEE EVERYBODY AS IMPORTANT

Everybody has something to offer to the kingdom of God. God has a purpose and a plan for everyone in His kingdom. There is a place of ministry somewhere for everybody. No matter who you are or where you've been, you are important to God's plan.

In the Book of Luke, we find two stories where Jesus modeled this. He reached out to those whom others thought were rejects. Those around Jesus would have never been seen with those people because they had bad reputations. But Jesus saw them as important.

Luke 19:1-10 says:
> *He entered Jericho and was passing through. And there was a man called by the name of Zacchaeus; he was a chief tax collector and he was rich. Zacchaeus was trying to see who Jesus was, and was unable because of the crowd, for he was small in stature. So he ran on ahead and climbed up into a sycamore tree*

# THE SHIFT

*in order to see Him, for He was about to pass through that way. When Jesus came to the place, He looked up and said to him, "Zacchaeus, hurry and come down, for today I must stay at your house." And he hurried and came down and received Him gladly. When they saw it, they all began to grumble, saying, "He has gone to be the guest of a man who is a sinner." Zacchaeus stopped and said to the Lord, "Behold, Lord, half of my possessions I will give to the poor, and if I have defrauded anyone of anything, I will give back four times as much." And Jesus said to him, "Today salvation has come to this house, because he, too, is a son of Abraham. For the Son of Man has come to seek and to save that which was lost."*

Luke 7:36-38 says:

*Now one of the Pharisees was requesting Him to dine with him, and He entered the Pharisee's house and reclined **at the table**. And there was a woman in the city who was a sinner; and when she learned that He was reclining **at the table** in the Pharisee's house, she brought an alabaster vial of perfume, and standing behind Him at His feet, weeping, she began to wet His feet with her tears, and kept wiping them with the hair of her head, and kissing His feet and anointing them with the perfume.*

Finally, verses 44-50 say:

> Turning toward the woman, He said to Simon, "Do you see this woman? I entered your house; you gave Me no water for My feet, but she has wet My feet with her tears and wiped them with her hair. You gave Me no kiss; but she, since the time I came in, has not ceased to kiss My feet. You did not anoint My head with oil, but she anointed My feet with perfume. For this reason I say to you, her sins, which are many, have been forgiven, for she loved much; but he who is forgiven little, loves little." Then He said to her, "Your sins have been forgiven." Those who were reclining **at the table** with Him began to say to themselves, "Who is this man who even forgives sins?" And He said to the woman, "Your faith has saved you; go in peace."

Who around you may others consider to be rejects? At one time in my life, I may have been considered one of those. But thankfully, people reached out to me, spent time with me, and loved me back into the fold. They showed me the real love of God and helped me understand and realize that my life mattered to God and to them. They demonstrated true interdependence and included me in their circle. It was at this point that I turned my back on my past and accepted the plan and call of God for my life.

## STEP 2: ACCEPT THAT GOD HAS GIFTED EVERYONE TO SERVE

Every born-again child of God has been given specific gifts from God, enabling them to serve in some capacity in the kingdom of God. No one has every gift. But everyone has *some* God-given gifts, including you! When believers use their gifts in service to God, their lives become fruitful and fulfilling in a personal way. However, their fruitfulness and fulfillment multiply as they become part of a ministry team and partner their gifts with the gifts of others.

First Peter 4:10 tells us: "As each one has received a *special* gift, employ it in serving one another as good stewards of the manifold grace of God." Likewise, Romans 12:6 says: "Since we have gifts that differ according to the grace given to us, *each of us is to exercise them accordingly.*"

Serving sometimes frustrates people, especially when they are unsure of what their gifts are. Too many times, when people feel this way, they just throw in the towel and quit. Eventually, if they are not involved in some capacity, they will leave the church. They may be serving in the wrong area of ministry. Since we know that all of us have gifts and all of us should be using them in the church ministry, maybe we need to be serving in another area of ministry. Interdependence says, "You matter to us, and there is a place of ministry here for you, so we are going to help you discover your gifts and your place on this team."

## STEP 3: RALLY AROUND A COMMON MISSION

Interdependence is not about "doing your own thing." Interdependence is not about making a name for yourself. It's about coming together to accomplish something much bigger than what you could ever do on your own.

*I: INTERDEPENDENCE*

---

# INDEPENDENCE WILL BRING DIVISION, WHICH WILL RESULT IN SUBTRACTION. INTERDEPENDENCE WILL BRING UNITY, WHICH WILL RESULT IN MULTIPLICATION.

---

In Genesis 11, we see a great story of a group of self-centered people who were only interested in making a name for themselves. They set out to build for "themselves" a city with a tower that would reach into heaven. "They said, 'Come, let us build for ourselves a city, and a tower whose top *will reach* into heaven, and let us make for ourselves a name, otherwise we will be scattered abroad over the face of the whole earth" (Genesis 11:4). Though they were working together, they were working as independent contractors. It was all about "themselves." This caught the attention of God, not because they were doing a good thing but because they had their own agendas and were more interested in making a name for themselves than they were in doing something great for God. This was nothing more than an independent spirit at work.

God didn't bless it; He stopped it:

## THE SHIFT

*The LORD came down to see the city and the tower which the sons of men had built. The LORD said, "Behold, they are one people, and they all have the same language. And this is what they began to do, and now nothing which they purpose to do will be impossible for them. Come, let Us go down and there confuse their language, so that they will not understand one another's speech." So the LORD scattered them abroad from there over the face of the whole earth; and they stopped building the city.* —Genesis 11:5-8

To experience the power of interdependence, there has to be a rallying point. That rallying point is the mission of the church. We are not trying to build a city for ourselves or make a name for ourselves. We are working to build and expand the kingdom of God. Our marching orders come from our mission. Our mission defines who we are and why we exist. If we preach and teach the mission of the church, people will be drawn to it like a magnet. People want to be a part of something bigger than themselves. When your church has a mission, and the people know what it is, they will rally around it and commit to using their gifts to partner together and see it accomplished.

Independence will bring division, which will result in subtraction. Interdependence will bring unity, which will result in multiplication. Interdependence takes place when all the parts are working together towards the same mission. It's like the motor in your

## I: INTERDEPENDENCE

car. It is made up of many different parts, and they each have their own role and purpose. When they are all functioning properly, the motor performs well and empowers the vehicle to take you to your desired destination. However, when one part begins to act independently from the others, the car breaks down and will leave you stranded by the side of the road.

I believe many churches are stranded by the side of the road. They can't seem to get it going. They change drivers (pastors), thinking that they are the problem, but many times the driver is not the problem. It's the fact that the church needs an overhaul. Sometimes a driver (or, in our case, a pastor) can diagnose the problem (if they are a mechanic) and get all the parts realigned and functioning interdependently. When this happens, that church can experience revitalization and, like the bones in the valley, can come alive and stand on its feet like a mighty army. But, for this to happen, there must be interdependence, and there must be a clear mission that serves as a rallying point.

At FWC, our mission is our rallying point:

> *"Family Worship Center is a community of Spirit-Filled believers committed to God's purpose of changing lives, by worshipping God, leading others to Jesus, and building unified teams to care for all in every stage of life."*

## STEP 4: GET BUSY AND GO TO WORK

Everyone has to do their part. Everyone has to carry part of this load. No one has to carry it all, but God expects everyone to do their part. As a pastor, it is my responsibility to preach, teach, and communicate the mission of the church consistently in order for our people to buy into and commit to it. We must also provide ongoing training and support so that our people are equipped for every good work and do not become burdened down by the work of ministry.

There is something about pastors that makes them think they have to have their hand in every detail of the church. When pastors function this way, they are leaning towards independence—like everything depends upon them. Some are micro-managers, and they literally suffocate their volunteers. If we are going to embrace interdependence, we are going to have to let each part do its work. If we are doing our part in communicating the mission, raising up leaders, providing training, and giving clear direction, then we have to let these people go and do the work. You can't stand over them and breathe down their necks. Let them go and use their gifts. Coaches train their players and correct their mistakes during practice. When it's game time, they let the team play.

The apostle Paul understood this very well. In Ephesians 4, Paul writes about what this process should look like:

> *But to each one of us grace was given according to the measure of Christ's gift. Therefore it says, "WHEN*

## I: INTERDEPENDENCE

*HE ASCENDED ON HIGH, HE LED CAPTIVE A HOST OF CAPTIVES, AND HE GAVE GIFTS TO MEN."*

*(Now this expression, "He ascended," what does it mean except that He also had descended into the lower parts of the earth? He who descended is Himself also He who ascended far above all the heavens, so that He might fill all things.) And He gave some as apostles, and some as prophets, and some as evangelists, and some as pastors and teachers, for the equipping of the saints for the work of service, to the building up of the body of Christ; until we all attain to the unity of the faith, and of the knowledge of the Son of God, to a mature man, to the measure of the stature which belongs to the fullness of Christ. As a result, we are no longer to be children, tossed here and there by waves and carried about by every wind of doctrine, by the trickery of men, by craftiness in deceitful scheming; but speaking the truth in love, we are to grow up in all aspects into Him who is the head, even Christ, from whom the whole body, being fitted and held together by what every joint supplies, according to the proper working of each individual part, causes the growth of the body for the building up of itself in love. —Ephesians 4:7-16*

If you are a pastor, then do the work of the pastor—"the equipping of the saints for the work of service, to the building up of the body of Christ; until we all attain to the unity of the faith, and of the knowledge of the Son of God, to a mature man, to

## THE SHIFT

the measure of the stature which belongs to the fullness of Christ" (vs. 12-13).

If you are a volunteer, then do the work you were equipped to do—"from whom the whole body, being fitted and held together by what every joint supplies, according to the proper working of each individual part, causes the growth of the body for the building up of itself in love" (v. 16).

Before we move on, let me give you a few final thoughts about interdependence:

**1) Work with the people you have, and trust God to send the people you need.**
People are not perfect, and neither are you. I have found that when we get people involved, they will grow. Don't wait until they get everything right in their lives. Give them a job and watch things in their lives change. Peter had serious flaws in his life, but Jesus chose him anyway. Judas . . . we all know about his demise, but Jesus chose to keep him on the team.

When we first planted FWC in 1994, I think almost everybody who came to church smoked. They actually had a "butt can" under the carport where they all went out and smoked between Sunday school and church. I could have made a big deal about it, preached against it, and shunned them, but I never mentioned it, even one time. I didn't preach against smoking or condemn them for doing it. Truthfully, the Bible talks more about gossiping than it does about smoking, so I just left it alone. A few months later, I noticed that the "butt can" was gone, and no one gathered under the carport to smoke anymore. God changed those people, not me. And now, thirty years later, some of those people have become the best leaders I've ever had.

**2) Everyone must take ownership of the church's mission.**
Most people do not have a mission for their lives. Therefore, I encourage them to make FWC's mission their mission. The transformation that takes place in your people is amazing when they have a mission. They take it personally. It empowers them to greater things. It gets them up in the morning with purpose and passion to accomplish something great for God. This inspires interdependence. They feel like they are a part of something bigger than themselves. They don't feel like they are doing life alone.

Does your church have an official written mission statement? If not, why not? If so, what is it? Do your people know it?

If your church does not have a mission statement, and you would like me to lead you through the process of defining your mission, scan the QR code to receive my free series, *The Mission*.

**3) Understand that every ministry is dependent upon another.**
Interdependence is all about doing ministry together, not alone. Though we may be serving in different areas of ministry, we are all on the same team. There are ministries in every church that everybody recognizes. The worship team, the choir, and the

## THE SHIFT

band are seen every week by those who attend church. The children's ministry is a big hit because parents are dropping their kids off every week. Women's ministries have raised thousands of dollars for multiple projects and are recognized regularly. But these ministries are not the only ministries in the church.

---

# WHEN ONE PERSON ACCEPTS JESUS INTO THEIR LIVES ON SUNDAY MORNING, EVERYBODY ON THE TEAM GETS CREDIT FOR IT.

---

We must shield ourselves from thinking that the ministry we are involved in is the most important ministry in the church. There are multiple ministries that, though not in the spotlight, are essential to the overall effectiveness of the church. The security team; the valets in the parking lot; the technical team running sound, lights, cameras, and the PowerPoint; those editing the livestream; the nursery workers; those who clean the building, mow the grass, serve the coffee, plus many more—they make what we see in the spotlight shine. Without these ministries, nothing we do in the spotlight would be worth watching. Interdependence says we are all a part of the whole. When one person accepts Jesus into their lives on Sunday morning, everybody on the team gets credit for it.

**4) Connect every person to the process of discipleship.**
Everybody doing ministry must receive ministry from somewhere in the church. Burnout is a real issue, and it is caused by putting out more than you are putting in. The reason people run out of gas in their vehicles is that they were too busy to stop and get gas. It is easy to get so involved in doing ministry that you neglect to take time to receive ministry.

Jesus, in some of His last words, instructed His disciples to go and make disciples (Matthew 28:19-20). That charge has now been given over to the church. Therefore, we should not only be making disciples, but we must also continue to become disciples ourselves.

Making disciples is a multifaceted assignment. It can take place in a traditional Sunday school setting, but it can also happen on a Zoom call with your team. It can happen in a Wednesday night Bible study or in a weekend training conference. It can be done in a staff meeting with your administrative team or over a cup of coffee with a team leader at the Waffle House. Whatever setting you choose, there should be teaching, training, practical application, questions, and answers that promote dialogue, accountability, and follow-through. I have learned in my years of discipling others that "If you are going to go together, you have to grow together."

## THE SHIFT

Interdependence is a key ingredient in creating an environment for transformation. Refuse to be an independent contractor. Refuse to do your own thing. Instead, choose to be a part of a ministry team using your gifts in tandem with other believers.

# CHAPTER 5
# F: FOCUS OUT

## F: FOCUS OUT

God has always had an external point of view when it relates to the harvest. Most churches and pastors have an internal point of view. I must confess that I have been guilty of this myself. I have at times been snagged by the numbers game, wanting to know, "How many did we have today?" "Why were we down twenty-five people from last Sunday?" "Are you sure you got the count right?" "I thought for sure we had more than that!"

I do believe that God is concerned with numbers, and I believe that we should be, as well. Numbers are a measuring tool for evaluation, and I think that we ought to be aware of how many were in the building on Sunday. But they can also be a trap. When the attendance is up and the building is full, we tend to think that we have really done something. Truthfully, the number of lost people outside of our building is far greater than the number we have inside. If we desire a SHIFT and real transformation to take place, we must focus out.

The words of Jesus are very clear, and His words echo the very heart of God throughout the New Testament.

# THE SHIFT

Matthew 28:19:
> "**Go therefore** and make disciples of all the nations, baptizing them in the name of the Father and the Son and the Holy Spirit."

Mark 16:15-16:
> "**Go into all the world** and preach the gospel to all creation. He who has believed and has been baptized shall be saved; but he who has disbelieved shall be condemned."

Acts 1:8:
> "But you will receive power when the Holy Spirit has come upon you; and **you shall be My witnesses** both in Jerusalem, and in all Judea and Samaria, and even **to the remotest part of the earth**."

Luke 14:16-17; 21-23:
> "A man was giving a big dinner, and **he invited many**; and at the dinner hour he sent his slave to say to those who had been invited, 'Come; for everything is ready now. . . .'
>
> "And the slave came back and reported this to his master. Then the head of the household became angry and said to his slave, '**Go out at once into the streets and lanes of the city** and bring in here the poor and crippled and blind and lame.' And the slave said, 'Master, what you commanded has been done, and still there is room.' And the master said to

the slave, '**Go out into the highways and along the hedges**, and compel them to come in, so that my house may be filled.'"

John 4:35:
> "Do you not say, 'There are yet four months, and then comes the harvest?' Behold, I say to you, **lift up your eyes and look on the fields**, that they are white for harvest."

My friend Dr. Wayne Lee says, "A pastor and a church will not be judged by what's in the barn, but instead by what's left in the field." As pastors and leaders, we must start thinking bigger than our church and our building. We have to think about our town. You must pastor your town and your community, not just the people that sit in your church every week. God wants to bring multiplication to your church, but it begins by focusing out on your entire town and community. It's time that we expand our borders and return to the highways and hedges. Isaiah instructs us to:

> "Enlarge the place of your tent;
> Stretch out the curtains of your dwellings, spare not;
> Lengthen your cords
> And strengthen your pegs.
> For you will spread abroad to the right and to the left.
> And your descendants will possess nations
> And will resettle the desolate cities."
> —Isaiah 54:2-3

# THE SHIFT

Jesus died to save the world. Most pastors are content to pastor their churches. We pray that God would send the harvest in. Jesus prayed that the Holy Spirit would send us out. It's time for us to lift up our eyes to the harvest in our town. Jesus said that the harvest is not coming; it is already here. We must focus O.U.T. in three steps.

## O: OPEN THE EYES OF OUR HEARTS TO SEE A HURTING WORLD

Paul, the great apostle, speaks of becoming *"all things to all people"* that he might win them. It's obvious he was not referring to those within, but those without:

> *For though I am free from all men, I have made myself a slave to all, so that I may win more. To the Jews I became as a Jew, so that I might win Jews; to those who are under the Law, as under the Law though not being myself under the Law, so that I might win those who are under the Law; to those who are without law, as without law, though not being without the law of God but under the law of Christ, so that I might win those who are without law. To the weak I became weak, that I might win the weak; I have become all things to all men, so that I may by all means save some. I do all things for the sake of the gospel, so that I may become a fellow partaker of it.*
> —*1 Corinthians 9:19-23*

Listen to that same passage from *The Message*:

> *Even though I am free of the demands and expectations of everyone, I have voluntarily become a servant to any and all in order to reach a wide range of people: religious, nonreligious, meticulous moralists, loose-living immoralists, the defeated, the demoralized—whoever. I didn't take on their way of life. I kept my bearings in Christ—but I entered their world and tried to experience things from their point of view. I've become just about every sort of servant there is in my attempts to lead those I meet into a God-saved life. I did all this because of the Message. I didn't just want to talk about it; I wanted to be in on it!*
> —*1 Corinthians 9:19-23*

Paul said that he *"entered their world and tried to experience things from their point of view."* Wow! How long has it been since we, as pastors, took a tour of our town—the neighborhoods and the country roads that are off the beaten path—the areas that few Christians want to go? When was the last time we stopped to talk to a stranger sitting at the stop sign on the corner, or standing in the parking lot at the old convenience store? We must open our eyes to see a hurting world, but we can't see it from our office desks. We must go to where they are.

In John 4, Jesus tells us not to put it off until later. He informs us that the time is now. We are great procrastinators. We're always waiting on the "right time." Jesus says, "Do you not say, 'There are yet four months, and *then* comes the harvest'? Behold, I say to you, lift up your eyes and look on the fields, that they are white for harvest" (John 4:35).

Jesus is our ultimate role model. He spent time in the temple. He spent time alone with His Father in prayer. He spent time alone with His disciples to teach and train them. But, when the teaching was finished, He said, "Let's go guys; we've got work to do," and He went to where the people were:

> *Jesus was going through all the cities and villages, teaching in their synagogues and proclaiming the gospel of the kingdom, and healing every kind of disease and every kind of sickness.*
> 
> *Seeing the people, He felt compassion for them, because they were distressed and dispirited like sheep without a shepherd.* —*Matthew 9:35-36*

In July of 1994, my wife Dianne and I, along with our two young sons, Joshua (two years old) and Jonathan (seven months old), moved to my hometown of Cairo, Georgia, to plant FWC. (Our daughter, Anna, didn't arrive until May of 1997.) We only had fourteen people in our first service, but we were thankful for every one of them. In January of 1995, we had a weekend leadership conference and invited all our people to come. We had twenty-five people show up, but it was at this conference that we worked through the process of redefining the mission of our church. The people caught it. They bought into it, and our church took on a new identity and began to grow. We now knew and understood who we were and why we existed. As I look back now, I realize that a SHIFT had occurred that weekend.

In March of 1995, during the first revival meeting that ever took place at FWC, evangelist Keith Barron gave a word of prophecy that said: *"Family Worship Center will become the hub of the wheel for a great move of God in this region."* Even today, thirty years later, we still hold to this word. We have seen and continue to see its fulfillment because we have opened our eyes to a community and region that needs God.

A few years later, my mentor, Dr. Wayne Lee, came to Cairo and spent a weekend with us. With years of experience as a successful pastor who built three megachurches, and as a vice president and professor at Southeastern University in Lakeland, Florida, he was very interested in our church. He was amazed at what he saw and felt at FWC. We spent hours talking that weekend and hardly slept at all. I had tons of questions for him, and he had about as many questions for me. Before he left that weekend, he looked me in the eye and said, *"You have got to start thinking bigger than Cairo. You have got to begin thinking about this region. God wants to bring multiplication to FWC throughout this entire region. You have to expand your borders fifty miles."* His words hit me in my core and reminded me of a plaque on my desk with the words of Isaiah's prophecy:

> *"Enlarge the place of your tent;*
> *Stretch out the curtains of your dwellings, spare not;*
> *Lengthen your cords*

# THE SHIFT

*And strengthen your pegs.*
*For you will spread abroad to the right and to the left.*
*And your descendants will possess nations*
*And will resettle the desolate cities."* —Isaiah 54:2

Think about this:

- » How many people drive more than ten miles to get to your church? Fifteen? Twenty? Twenty-five? Thirty? More than thirty?
- » The town they live in is part of God's plan too.
- » What is our role as a church to begin making a difference in their areas?

---

## IF WE ARE GOING TO FOCUS OUT, WE MUST OPEN THE EYES OF OUR HEARTS TO SEE A HURTING WORLD.

---

My dear friend and mentor Pastor Benny Tate of Rock Springs Church in Milner, Georgia, has been a great example to me of what it means to focus out. He and his church have truly modeled what it means to open your heart to see a hurting world. A friend of mine told me that I needed to see his church. He said,

"It is in the middle of nowhere, but thousands of people attend every week." I thought, *No way is that happening!*

I'll never forget the first time I pulled up at his church. I could hardly believe what I saw. The city limit sign said, "Milner, GA, Population 684." My GPS didn't even know how to get me to the church. When I finally found the church, I couldn't believe what I saw. My friend was right. This church IS Milner, GA. There's nothing else there. When I walked in and met Pastor Benny Tate for the first time, I knew why this church was so effective. This man has a genuine heart for people, and he has opened his heart to see a hurting world. Even though they average eight thousand people on their campus every Sunday, this meant nothing to him. What meant more to him than anything was the harvest in the field that needed to be reaped. This man and his church work the field. Every day, he is in the community and the neighboring communities round about him. He walks among the people. He visits with them, eats with them, honors them, recognizes them, gives to them, and truly ministers to them.

Obviously, the majority of the people who attend his church drive in from the surrounding areas simply because he has taught his church to focus out. As they have done this, gradually, over time, their borders have expanded. He has led by example, and in doing so, they have enlarged the place of their tent. They have stretched out the curtains of their dwellings. They have spared not. They have lengthened their cords and have strengthened their pegs. This has caused them to spread abroad to the right and to the left. And their people are possessing nations and are resettling the desolate cities. If we are going to focus out, we must open the eyes of our hearts to see a hurting world.

## U: UTILIZE EVERY TOOL WE HAVE AT OUR DISPOSAL

The greatest tool any church has is its people. When people accept Jesus into their lives, they are excited about what has just happened to them, and they are eager to learn and grow in this new life. At some point, they begin to realize that God's hand is upon them. Soon, they sense a prodding on the inside that there must be something God wants them to do. What they need is a pastor and a church to equip them, to train them to do ministry, and then release them into the body to use their gifts and do meaningful ministry.

Sadly, in many churches, this doesn't happen. Recently, I had a conversation with a young adult named, Morgan, who has been attending FWC for a little over a year. Though she was raised in church, she didn't accept Christ into her life until she came to FWC. After accepting Christ and being baptized, she joined the church—and the choir and worship team. In our conversation, she told me that she had recently read my book *HomeGrown: Growing What You Have Where You Are*.[20] She was so intrigued by it that she couldn't put it down. She shared that she had no idea that growing a church was "a thing." She said, *"Growing up, we just attended church. I thought that was all we were supposed to do. I knew nothing about growing in my relationship with God, finding and using my spiritual gifts,*

---

20 Johnny Moore, *HomeGrown: Growing What You Have Where You Are* (Stockbridge, GA: Dream Releaser Publishing, 2024).

*getting involved in ministry, and reaching other people for Christ."* I believe that many people are sitting in churches every week who are just like Morgan.

The greatest asset that any church has is its people. If we are going to experience a SHIFT that will lead to a transformation, we must focus out! This has to start with the people sitting in our church every week. They are the greatest tools we have for evangelism. We have to teach them, train them, challenge them, and empower them to connect with and reach those in their circle of life. This is exactly what the apostle Paul was referring to when he said:

> *I didn't take on their way of life. I kept my bearings in Christ—but I entered their world and tried to experience things from their point of view. I've become just about every sort of servant there is in my attempts* ***to lead those I meet into a God-saved life.***
> *—1 Corinthians 9:22 (MSG)*

---

# FOCUSING OUT IS NOT ABOUT KEEPING PEOPLE OUT. FOCUSING OUT IS ABOUT FIGURING OUT HOW TO GET PEOPLE IN.

---

# THE SHIFT

We also have our facilities and property as additional tools. Most churches sit empty more than they are used. I have found that our facilities and properties can be used as tools to focus out. As pastors, we want to see cars pulling in the parking lot and people walking into our buildings. However, we are only focusing on Sundays and Wednesdays. What about the other five days of the week? Pastor Benny Tate says, *"Never underestimate the power of getting people on your property and in your building."* His thinking is, if you can get people used to coming to your church for funerals, banquets, weddings, baby showers, birthday parties, or other non-church related events, they will feel more comfortable coming when you invite them to church on Sunday.

Focusing out is not about keeping people out. Focusing out is about figuring out how to get people in. The object is to get the harvest out of the field and into the barn. Let me explain.

Living in a farming community, I have seen firsthand how farmers work. Cole Prince, one of the biggest farmers in our community and a member of FWC, told me that when peanuts are ready, they dig them up and leave them lying in the field for three to four days to let them dry. But, on the fourth day, they go harvest them and take them to the peanut mill, where they are cleaned and dried if they are still damp. If there is rain in the forecast, they get them out of the field before the rain comes in order to keep from paying the mill more money to dry and clean them.

Three takeaways from Farmer Cole:

1) **When the harvest is ready, it must be reaped.** When the harvest is ready, there is nothing more important than reaping it. Everything else is put on hold. Everyone's attention is turned to the harvest. Leaving it in the field, even one day too long, could risk losing the harvest completely. This is why Jesus told His disciples, "You know the saying, 'Four months between planting and harvest.' But I say, wake up and look around. The fields are already ripe for harvest" (John 4:35, NLT).

2) **The longer the harvest lies in the field, the more difficult it is to clean it up and dry it out.** The elements have a way of affecting the harvest. When the harvest is ready, it has to be collected. I have seen tractors, combines, peanut-pickers and cotton-pickers, hay-balers, semis, and all kinds of equipment in the fields at all hours of the night. Those fields would be lit up like a football stadium. The reason? The harvest is ready, the rain is coming, and the harvest has to be reaped, now. When we neglect the harvest for whatever reason, it hardens. It's harder to clean. It's harder to dry out. Think about this in regard to the "people" harvest. Nothing is too hard for God, but is it possible that the reason so many people struggle with overcoming addictions and dysfunctional behaviors is because we left them in the field too long? Just a thought!

3) **When the harvest is ready, get it out of the field and into the barn.** The purpose of reaching the harvest is not to leave it in the field. The purpose of reaching the harvest

# THE SHIFT

is to get it into the barn or the storehouse. When we talk about reaching the harvest—the lost and the outcast—it is not to leave them in the field where we found them. Our mission is to get them into the storehouse—the church! This is where the Holy Spirit can clean them up and dry them out. It's the place where the church can disciple them, train them, and prepare them to follow us back into the harvest field to do the same for others.

This is why we should see our facilities and our properties as tools to focus out. At FWC, we open our doors to all kinds of events and functions. We host our high school football team for dinner during football season. We host award banquets for the high school baseball team, the basketball team, a local dance company, and others. Earlier this year, we hosted the annual fundraising banquet for the Jackie Robinson Boys and Girls Club. The keynote speaker for the event was baseball Hall of Famer Chipper Jones. There were hundreds of people there, not to hear me preach, but to see the great Chipper Jones. But, because we used our building as a tool to get people in the door, some who were at that banquet have since come to church at FWC.

Our property is another tool we have used. We have been blessed with thirty-two acres on the main four-lane that comes into Cairo. The first thing you see when you come into the city limits of Cairo from the west is FWC. We have a five-acre tract of land on the west side of our property. In February of 2022, we began what we called "The CrossFit Project." We erected a huge 120-foot cross on those five acres. The cross is lit up and can be seen from any direction, even before you see the church—day or night. It is absolutely beautiful! After we completed the cross, we built a quarter-mile walking track around it. It is landscaped beautifully, and we have used that property for all types of events, such as Easter egg hunts, Easter sunrise services, Fourth of July concerts and fireworks, fall festivals, church picnics, weddings, and other things. All these events have brought unchurched people to our campus, who would never have come without using this property as a tool. But, on top of all of this, the walking track has become a huge gathering place for our community. People from our community come to this track to walk every day. I have seen people there at all hours of the day and night. My point is this: One day, they may walk in the door on Sunday.

Here's one final thought—when it comes to reaching family and friends, there are specific church events that will get them in the door that Easter and Christmas will not. I'm referring to baby dedications, water baptisms, and church membership. Unbelievers will come to church to watch their families and friends dedicate babies, get baptized, and join the church, when they wouldn't come any other time. Plan these events. Prepare for them. Send "Save the Date" cards from the church to their families and friends. You will be amazed at who will walk in the door if you take advantage of these opportunities to focus out.

# THE SHIFT

## T: TAKE THE MINISTRY OF THE CHURCH TO THE STREETS

The gospel was always meant for the streets. In the Book of Acts, miracles, signs, and wonders took place in the streets more than they did in the temple. Peter and John healed the man at the gate in the street, not in the temple. But when he received his miracle, he immediately went to the temple! We cannot wait for people to enter our doors before we share the gospel with them. We have to go where they are.

The apostle Paul, as we read earlier, said that he entered **their** world and tried to experience things from **their** point of view. He went to where they were. He continued by saying, "When I am with those who are weak, I share their weakness, for I want to bring the weak to Christ. Yes, **I try to find common ground with everyone, doing everything I can to save some**" (1 Corinthians 9:22, NLT). Again, he is not in the temple but the streets. I love the way he ends this passage: "I did all this because of the Message. I didn't just want to talk about it; **I wanted to be *in* on it!**" (1 Corinthians 9:23, MSG) Can you see his excitement? He said, *I could not keep this to myself! I had to take it to the streets!*

At FWC, we have ministries that take the ministry to the streets. We have ministries that go to the nursing homes and ministries that visit the hospitals and pray for those in need. We have ministries that reach out to the schools, especially to the faculty and staff. We have ministries that provide meals for the high school's sports teams and the high school band throughout the year. We have ministries that are connected to law enforcement and ministries that reach out to the homeless and the needy in our community. We have ministries that focus on assistance with utilities, rent, and other needs. We have ministries that provide home-cooked meals for shut-ins and others in need. However, I am of the opinion that there is a greater way to take the ministry of the church to the streets.

We have all been called to the highways and hedges to share the gospel. But what exactly does that mean? This means a lot of different things to different churches. For some, it would mean having an Evangelism 101 class and teaching people how to share their faith. For others, it would mean memorizing the Roman Road plan and the ABCs of Salvation, and then meeting at 10:00 on Saturday morning and going out two by two to knock on doors. If that's what you feel good about doing, then I would say go for it. But, as I read the Scriptures, Jesus's approach was much more personal and "hands-on." His method was not like a scripted telemarketer spouting off something that was memorized when the homeowner answers the door.

What I do see, however, is the model that Jesus gave included seeing the people where they were, showing compassion to those who were hurting and broken, and providing direction to those who were lost and couldn't find their way. Matthew writes concerning this model and explains that Jesus, "Seeing the people, He felt compassion for them because they were distressed and dispirited like sheep without a shepherd" (Matthew 9:36). Jesus became a Shepherd to them. He met them where they were, showed compassion in the area of their need, and helped guide them into the fold.

# THE SHIFT

We see this same pattern in Luke 15 when Jesus gives the parable of the lost sheep:

> *"If a man has a hundred sheep and one of them gets lost, what will he do? Won't he leave the ninety-nine others in the wilderness and go to search for the one that is lost until he finds it? And when he has found it, he will joyfully carry it home on his shoulders."*
> —Luke 15:4-5 (NLT)

Notice that when the shepherd found the lost sheep, he didn't leave it where he found it; he brought it home, or back into the fold. I think it's important for us to understand that when we focus out, and in this case, take the gospel to the streets, that our ultimate goal is not to just meet their immediate need. We may have to meet their need to get their attention, but our goal is not to just feed them and leave them where they are. Our goal is to get them into the fold. Our goal is always to "make disciples."

When it comes to taking it to the streets, Jesus told his disciples, "The harvest is plentiful, but the workers are few. Therefore beseech the Lord of the harvest to send out workers into His harvest" (Matthew 9:37-38). Jesus said, "Pray that the Lord of the harvest would send laborers into the harvest" (author paraphrase). All of us who are a part of the church should be laborers in the harvest. None of us actually lives at the church. We all live elsewhere, and most of us go to work every day. We go to the grocery store, the restaurant, the ballpark, the gym, the gas station, the barbershop, the beauty salon, the bank, the post office, the school, the dance studio, and on and on and on. Listen, we are in the street—the harvest field—every day! But we're not focused out—we're focused in. We walk by hurting people every day. We walk through the harvest every day. We simply need to follow Jesus's model and do what He did:

- » **We see them.** If we are focused out, we will see them. They are everywhere. They are hurting. They are worried. They are fearful. They are broken. They have no purpose. When we stop and reach out to them, we are taking the ministry of the church to the streets.
- » **We have compassion on them.** Compassion is not feeling sorry for someone. Compassion is "love in action." We minister to them by meeting their need if we can do so. Peter and John, at the gate Beautiful, told the man, "We don't have what you want, but we do have what you need" (Acts 3:2-8). You may not be able to give them what they want, but you do have what they need. Pray for them. Encourage them. Tell them Jesus loves them, and that's why He sent you across their path.
- » **We give them direction.** We become a shepherd in their lives for a moment, and we point them to the church. We don't want to leave the harvest in the field or the sheep in the wilderness. We want to get the harvest in the barn and the sheep in the fold.

We are all in the harvest field every day. Imagine what would happen if we began to focus out instead of focus in. It very well could be what we need for a SHIFT to occur. The miraculous happens when the church begins to focus out.

As I close this chapter, I want to give you five steps that we use to help us focus out:

**1) We challenge everybody to invite someone to church every week.**
The greatest way to get those on the outside in is to invite them to come. This really isn't as hard as it seems, and you would be surprised how many would come if someone actually asked them. Focusing out is about awareness. Being aware of who God brings across your path. We have to train ourselves and our people to be aware of God's leading throughout the day. Have you ever pulled away from the gas station and thought, *Shoot, I should have invited that person next to me to church!* Developing this awareness comes from keeping this challenge in front of your people every week.

**2) We schedule four big events at the church every year.**
Churches are known for events. Churches are always planning revivals, gospel sings, homecomings, and other church-related events. We must not become a church that is event-driven. We must be mission-driven. Every event we schedule must be mission-driven. Planning a big church event every month is just too much. It wears on our volunteers and keeps us busy doing frivolous work. Obviously, different ministries of the church plan events and outings for their specific ministries, and this is good. It builds community among those involved, promotes fellowship,

and develops relationships. But when it comes to church events, we focus on four big events per year: Easter, Back-to-School Sunday, I Love This Church Day, and Christmas. These events are designed to focus out. We are reaching unchurched people, and all our efforts are geared towards getting the unchurched into the building. All our ministries partner together to make these four events the greatest experience that unchurched people have ever had with church.

### 3) We implement a 90-60-30-day outreach plan.

When planning big events, you can't wait until the last two weeks before the event to plan it. The event will never be successful, and your people will be discouraged because it wasn't effective like they hoped it would be. To effectively focus out, you have to plan at least ninety days out. When we hit the ninety-day window, we begin promoting the event internally. We share the event, define the purpose and the goal of the event, and recruit the entire church to begin praying for the success of the event. We also begin meeting with team leaders to assist us in the planning and facilitation of the event. We need all the volunteers on board. By the time we hit the sixty-day window, the event is planned, the teams are in place, and we begin to focus on who we want to reach. We challenge our people to decide who they want to invite and what their strategy will be to get them here. We use church consultant Thom Rainer's method of *"Who is your One?"*[21] Choose the one person or the one family you want to reach and do everything you can to get them here.

---

21 Thom S. Rainer, *I Am a Church Member: Discovering the Attitude That Makes the Difference* (Nashville, TN: B&H Publishing Groups, 2013).

## THE SHIFT

At the sixty-day point, we encourage our people to show random acts of kindness towards those they are targeting. Reach out to them. Send them a message that you are thinking about them. Let them know that you are praying for them. When we reach the thirty-day window, we begin throwing the net. We create invite cards and make them available to our people to use to invite their "one." We go the extra mile to provide resources to our people to help them get their family and friends in the door. A couple of weeks out from the event, we have a volunteer rally where we meet with all our volunteers to thank them for their help, cover any last-minute details, and answer any questions or concerns that they may have. We end the rally with a time of prayer and celebration for all.

**4) We advertise and promote our church in the community.**
Advertising and promoting your church in the community is essential to focusing out. We believe it is important to let the community know what is taking place at FWC. We love our town and our community, and we want them to know that what we offer at FWC has the potential to make our community better. Some churches shy away from advertising for fear of promoting themselves. I think this is a mistake. Advertising is not about promoting yourself; it's about communicating what God is doing at your church with others in your area of reach.

The woman at the well was the first person to use social media. When she had an encounter with Jesus, she immediately returned to her community and proclaimed, "Come, see a man who told me all the things that I *have* done; this is not the Christ, is it?" They went out of the city, and were coming to Him" (John 4:29-30). This was advertising! If you have a product that has the potential to change lives, why would you want to keep it to yourself?

We began using advertising at FWC two weeks before we planted the church in 1994. At that time, it was unheard of for a church to advertise in the local newspaper. There were no social media platforms in those days—only word of mouth and *The Cairo Messenger*. We advertised every week in the newspaper. When I walked through the community, people would say, "Congratulations on the new church. I saw it in the paper. I'll have to come out and visit with you one Sunday." Some of them came, and some of them didn't, but the good news was, they knew we were here.

Since those early days in 1994, we have increased our advertising in multiple ways. Social media has changed the face of advertising, and in that respect, has been extremely beneficial for the church. We post daily on all the social media platforms and have been able to reach and connect with thousands of people through our posts and our livestream. We advertise on the electronic billboards and rent a banner display across Broad Street for our big events. And, for those who are still old school, we buy advertisements in the local newspaper. We've created customized FWC yard signs, and they are planted in people's yards all over our region. Our *HomeBrood Store* at FWC has all kinds of novelty items and FWC merchandise such as hats, t-shirts, hoodies and sweatshirts, candles, car decals, and other items. People have enjoyed these items, and they wear them and display them proudly.

Advertising costs money, but we have learned that it is money well spent. If you reach one family and they get involved and begin tithing and giving, the advertising just paid for itself. We also want everyone in the community to recognize the FWC name. When people in our town think "church," we want them to think "Family Worship Center."

**5) We are committed to reaching our "Jerusalem harvest."**
As I have already said, focusing out is a major part of creating the SHIFT. Jesus instructed us to go into all the world and make disciples. In His final words to His disciples, He gave them a mandate: "You will receive power when the Holy Spirit has come upon you; and you shall be My witnesses both in Jerusalem, and in all Judea and Samaria, and even to the remotest part of the earth" (Acts 1:8, emphasis added). We are a supporter of world missions and committed to reaching the world with the gospel of Jesus Christ. But I believe we are responsible for our "Jerusalem harvest" first. In Matthew 16:24, we find the great discipleship passage where Jesus cuts to the chase and tells it like it is: "If you're going to follow Me, then you're going to have to deny yourself, take up your cross, and follow Me!" (author paraphrase) He lays it out, plain and simple.

While this whole passage is challenging, He makes a statement that has always struck a chord with me. He says, "For what will it profit a man if he gains the whole world and forfeits his soul?

Or what will a man give in exchange for his soul?" (Matthew 16:26) When I think about this scripture, I can't help but think about my family and my community. If I win the whole world at the expense of my own family or community, what profit is it? If I focus my attention on the whole world and allow those next door or across the street to go to hell, was there any profit to it?

---

## WHAT DOES IT PROFIT A MAN IF HE REACHES THE WHOLE WORLD BUT FORFEITS HIS JERUSALEM HARVEST?

---

When God has called someone as a pastor to a local community, I believe your first responsibility is to those who live where you serve. If God has called you to world missions, then your first responsibility is to those where you serve. Where you serve becomes your Jerusalem harvest. As pastors and churches, we should support those who are called to the uttermost parts of the earth, but our primary responsibility is to our Jerusalem harvest. What does it profit a man if he reaches the whole world but forfeits his Jerusalem harvest?

My Jerusalem harvest is Cairo, Georgia, and the surrounding area. This is where God has called me, and this is where I serve. When Jesus looked at His Jerusalem, He wept. He wept because

## THE SHIFT

He knew what was coming, and He knew they weren't ready. We should weep over our Jerusalem for the same reason. God loves the people of my town and my community, and He gave His son to die for them. If your heart doesn't break for your town and community, and if you're not willing to focus out and reach those where you are, then maybe where you are is not where you're supposed to be.

# CHAPTER 6
# T: TRANSFORMATION

## T: TRANSFORMATION

The word "transformation" is a biblical word. It is the spiritual process whereby men, women, boys, and girls are changed into the persons God intended them to be. It's what happens when a sinner becomes a saint, a child of darkness becomes a child of light, and a dead-end road becomes the birthplace of your destiny. The apostle Paul had a revelation about transformation, and he wrote about it often.

1 Corinthians 15:51 (NLT):
*"But let me reveal to you a wonderful secret. We will not all die, but we will all be transformed!"*

Romans 12:2:
*"And do not be conformed to this world, but be transformed by the renewing of your mind, so that you may prove what the will of God is, that which is good and acceptable and perfect."*

2 Corinthians 3:18:
*"But we all, with unveiled face, beholding as in a mirror the glory of the Lord, are being transformed into the same image from glory to glory, just as from the Lord, the Spirit."*

# THE SHIFT

The word "transform" means *"to change in form, appearance, or structure."*[22] The Greek word used in these verses above is the word, *metamorphoo*, which, according to *Strong's Concordance* means *"to change, transfigure, or transform."*[23]

*Metamorphoo* is where we get our English word *metamorphose*. Metamorphose is defined as *"to change into a different physical form especially by supernatural means."*[24] The process of metamorphose happens from the inside out. It's the process whereby the caterpillar becomes the butterfly.

This process of transformation that happens from the inside out, like metamorphose, is what Jesus's conversation with Nicodemus was all about. Nicodemus was confused and wrestling with what was different between him and Jesus. He knew that Jesus was obviously a man sent from God because of all the signs and wonders that were taking place through Him. Listen to the conversation:

> *Now there was a man of the Pharisees, named Nicodemus, a ruler of the Jews; this man came to Jesus by night and said to Him, "Rabbi, we know that You have come from God as a teacher; for no one can do these signs that You do unless God is with him." Jesus answered and said to him, "Truly, truly, I say to you, unless one is born again he cannot see the kingdom of God."*

---

22 Dictionary.com, s.v. "transform," https://www.dictionary.com/browse/transform.
23 Strong's Concordance, s.v. "transform," https://biblehub.com/greek/3339.htm.
24 Dictionary.com, s.v. "metamorphose," https://www.merriam-webster.com/dictionary/metamorphose.

> *Nicodemus said to Him, "How can a man be born when he is old? He cannot enter a second time into his mother's womb and be born, can he?" Jesus answered, "Truly, truly, I say to you, unless one is born of water and the Spirit he cannot enter into the kingdom of God. That which is born of the flesh is flesh, and that which is born of the Spirit is spirit. Do not be amazed that I said to you, 'You must be born again.'"* —John 3:1-7

Jesus told him that he needed to be born again. He needed a transformation. Nicodemus was trying to understand this with his human reasoning, but he couldn't figure it out. Jesus explained to him that to see and experience the kingdom of God, not only must a man be born of flesh, but he must also be born of the Spirit. Transformation is a work of the Holy Spirit that begins on the inside and then works its way out.

When I read Ezekiel's story of the dry bones, I see something that had potential but is now dead. The bones needed a transformation. I believe some churches need a transformation. It's heartbreaking listening to pastors talk about their passion to grow and expand the kingdom, but their churches are like these bones. Just a faint remembrance of what used to be. God asked Ezekiel, "Can these bones live again?" Ezekiel answered like most pastors, "Oh, Lord God, only you know!" (Ezekiel 37:3, author paraphrase) The real answer is, "Yes, they can live again!" Your church can live again and stand up on its feet like a mighty army! But it's going to take a SHIFT for it to happen. When the SHIFT occurs, it will cause a transformation to take place—an internal

# THE SHIFT

work of the Holy Spirit. If we, as pastors, will work on the SHIFT, the Holy Spirit will bring the transformation.

Now, with this in mind, let's read the story again:

> *The hand of the LORD was upon me, and He brought me out by the Spirit of the LORD and set me down in the middle of the valley; and it was full of bones. He caused me to pass among them round about, and behold, there were very many on the surface of the valley; and lo, they were very dry. He said to me, "Son of man, can these bones live?" And I answered, "O Lord GOD, You know." Again He said to me, "Prophesy over these bones and say to them, 'O dry bones, hear the word of the LORD.' Thus says the Lord GOD to these bones, 'Behold, I will cause breath to enter you that you may come to life. I will put sinews on you, make flesh grow back on you, cover you with skin and put breath in you that you may come alive; and you will know that I am the LORD.'*
>
> *So I prophesied as I was commanded; and as I prophesied, there was a noise, and behold, a rattling; and the bones came together, bone to its bone. And I looked, and behold, sinews were on them, and flesh grew and skin covered them; but there was no breath in them. Then He said to me, "Prophesy to the breath, prophesy, son of man, and say to the breath, 'Thus says the Lord GOD, "Come from the four winds, O breath, and breathe on these slain, that they come*

*to life."'" So I prophesied as He commanded me, and the breath came into them, and they came to life and stood on their feet, an exceedingly great army.*

*Then He said to me, "Son of man, these bones are the whole house of Israel; behold, they say, 'Our bones are dried up and our hope has perished. We are completely cut off.' Therefore prophesy and say to them, 'Thus says the Lord GOD, "Behold, I will open your graves and cause you to come up out of your graves, My people; and I will bring you into the land of Israel. Then you will know that I am the LORD, when I have opened your graves and caused you to come up out of your graves, My people. I will put My Spirit within you and you will come to life, and I will place you on your own land. Then you will know that I, the LORD, have spoken and done it," declares the LORD.'"*
—Ezekiel 37:1-14

God is speaking here about a transformation of a whole nation of people. If God can bring a transformation to a whole nation, certainly He can bring a transformation to your church! A church "transformation" is the result of a divine SHIFT that causes all of the pieces to come together in their proper place, resulting in new life, renewed purpose, new vision, and fresh passion and power to accomplish the perfect will of God, thus creating an environment for a transformation.

When pastors start working the process that I have laid out for the SHIFT, it doesn't take long before they see signs that a transformation is approaching. Like rain clouds forming in the distance that let you know the rain is coming, God gives us signs that a transformation is on the horizon. There are four signs that a transformation is taking place.

## SIGN 1: THE CHURCH BEGINS LIVING FROM THE INSIDE OUT

Churches are driven by many different things. Tradition, personalities, money, fads, programs, and other things are the driving forces behind many churches. But when you begin to see and hear your congregation talking about mission and vision, you can tell that the tide is turning. A mission-driven church lives from the inside out. A mission-driven church draws its identity from the God who lives inside of its people. Living from the outside in produces unhappy and angry people and churches. They feel guarded, victimized, and paralyzed. Sinners are looked down upon and made to feel unwelcome.

---

> **IF THE CHURCH LOVES AND WELCOMES THOSE NOBODY WANTS, GOD WILL TRANSFORM THEM INTO PEOPLE OTHERS WOULD DIE TO HAVE.**

---

But the mission trumps everything when churches live from the inside out. The church extends their arms to the lost and hurting. They are not concerned about where these people have been or what they have done. They are not afraid of the world they live in because they know that "You are of God, little children, and have overcome them; because greater is He who is in you than he who is in the world" (1 John 4:4, BSB). They have an understanding that people matter to God, so they matter to us. When the people in a church live from the inside out, they discover solutions to problems, they become a church filled with joy, and they begin to experience real effectiveness and fruitfulness. All of these are signs that a transformation is forming.

## SIGN 2: THE CHURCH BEGINS LOVING FROM THE OUTSIDE IN

When churches begin loving and caring for people outside of their four walls, you know something is going on. When churches start loving from the outside in, it is proof that they are living from the inside out. They are becoming mission-driven. But our goal is not to just love them. We want to get them in the door! The fact that a church invites those from the outside in is a sure sign that it is moving in the right direction.

People on the outside need a church like ours. They need a place to belong, a place to learn and grow, and a place to experience the love of God. When the community begins to see that the church's mindset is "whosoever will let them come," this news will travel fast, and the unexpected will begin to show up. When our people start personifying the mission by inviting those who cross their path, you might be surprised who begins showing up.

## THE SHIFT

If the church loves and welcomes those nobody wants, God will transform them into people others would die to have.

One thing I have noticed about loving from the outside in is that those who at one time appeared to be enemies of the church will come. When a church just loves people, it's hard for the world to grasp, so they talk negatively about you. They will judge you. They will persecute you for righteousness's sake. I have learned that people are usually against what they don't understand. But Jesus said in His famous Sermon on the Mount:

> *"But I say to you who hear, love your enemies, do good to those who hate you, bless those who curse you, pray for those who mistreat you. Whoever hits you on the cheek, offer him the other also; and whoever takes away your coat, do not withhold your shirt from him either. Give to everyone who asks of you, and whoever takes away what is yours, do not demand it back. Treat others the same way you want them to treat you. If you love those who love you, what credit is that to you? For even sinners love those who love them. . . . But love your enemies, and do good, and lend, expecting nothing in return; and your reward will be great, and you will be sons of the Most High; for He Himself is kind to ungrateful and evil men."*
> —Luke 6:27-32, 35

This is what loving from the outside in looks like. When you can feel the excitement from the congregation when new people are coming, you can know that a transformation is approaching.

## SIGN 3: THE CHURCH BEGINS LABORING FROM THE INSIDE OUT

It becomes obvious that the church is making progress when they begin locking arms with one another and doing ministry together. Transformation is about realizing that God expects the church to be the body of Christ and do ministry—and He expects us to do it together, as a body. John Maxwell says, "The smartest person in the room is not as smart as everybody in the room when they are working as a team."[25] I love this! But here is my revision to the quote: *"The senior pastor of the church is not nearly as effective as all of the believers in the room when they are working together as a body."*

The pastor has God-given gifts, but he doesn't have all of them. All believers in the church have God-given gifts as well, but nobody has all of them. When the body's gifts are united, every gift the church needs is present. When the body works together as intended by God, ministry begins to overflow out of the four walls into the community. This is what Paul was pointing out in his first letter to the Corinthian church:

> *What then is Apollos? And what is Paul? Servants through whom you believed, even as the Lord gave*

---

25 John C. Maxwell, *Everyone Communicates, Few Connect: What the Most Effective People Do Differently* (Nashville, TN: Thomas Nelson, 2010), 45.

> *opportunity to each one. I planted, Apollos watered, but God was causing the growth. So then neither the one who plants nor the one who waters is anything, but God who causes the growth. Now he who plants and he who waters are one; but each will receive his own reward according to his own labor. For we are God's fellow workers; you are God's field, God's building.* —1 Corinthians 3:5-9

The issue is not "Who gets the credit?" The issue is "Did ministry happen, and were needs met?" God brought the increase, and He gets the credit.

We don't have to see eye to eye about everything—we just have to be focused on the same mission and vision. We have to be going in the same direction. Our hearts have to want the same things, to see the mission fulfilled and ministry happen to those in need in our community. When the church begins to labor from the inside out, it is a sure sign of a coming transformation.

## SIGN 4: THE CHURCH BEGINS LIFTING FROM THE OUTSIDE IN

The winds and storms of life affect every church. Truthfully, most of the time, they affect us negatively. However, there is no reason to be afraid when the storms come—and they WILL come. When the flood waters rise, the storm will cause you to rise if you are in the ship. What came to destroy you will develop you, and when the storm passes, you will discover that you are farther along than you were before the storm.

*T: TRANSFORMATION*

# THOUGH THE ENEMY COMES TO WREAK HAVOC IN THE LIVES OF PEOPLE, THE CHURCH BECOMES THE DOOR TO THOSE WHO ARE PERISHING.

Trouble and panic in our world will cause many to run to the church for help. But, unlike Noah, who could not open the door to those who were knocking, we can point them to the door. Jesus said, "I am the door; if anyone enters through Me, he will be saved, and will go in and out and find pasture. The thief comes only to steal and kill and destroy; I came that they may have life, and have it abundantly" (John 10:9-10). Though the enemy comes to wreak havoc in the lives of people, the church becomes the door to those who are perishing. We have been empowered to provide the lift to the downtrodden. This lift comes from the outside in.

When the SHIFT is occurring, the problems will lift the church, not cause it to fall. We can face every obstacle knowing that God is going to work all things for our good. We can be confident knowing that we will have the solution to every problem we face because we are a church on a mission. God's plan is for us to represent Christ and to make a difference in this world, and that includes our town and our community. As the storm around us

## THE SHIFT

rages, we will rise. Our influence will increase. Ministry opportunities will open. More volunteers will walk through the door. New leaders will be raised up. Resources will begin to flourish. God will provide everything you need, and you will begin to lift from the outside in.

To those who tried to cause us harm, we can say like Joseph, "As for you, you meant evil against me, *but* God meant it for good in order to bring about this present result, to preserve many people alive" (Genesis 50:20). So, don't be discouraged when trouble comes—rejoice! The SHIFT is on, and your church is standing on the threshold of a transformation!

# CHAPTER 7
# CREATING A SHIFT

In the beginning of this book, I shared about a dream God had given me concerning the SHIFT. I want to share the word God spoke to me one more time:

> "'I am bringing a shift to FWC. This shift will lift FWC to a new place and a new level. It will open the door to a great harvest that has only been seen in your heart. You will soon see it with your eyes. Prepare the people for the harvest that I am sending, for it is soon to come. Then you will know that I, the Lord, have spoken and done it,' declares the Lord." (7/27/2013 6:00 a.m.)

Notice the date that this dream took place—July 27, 2013. What I am about to tell you is not happenstance. I just discovered it myself in this moment. As I am writing right now, the date is July 27, 2025. This word from the Lord came to me exactly twelve years ago today!

As I pondered on this dream and word from the Lord early that morning (twelve years ago), these five components for the SHIFT came to me in a matter of minutes. But it took me a few months to process all of this for myself and my church. I knew God had given me something that would work and produce fruit. In January of 2014, we began to implement the SHIFT at FWC. Over the

# THE SHIFT

next few months, we began to experience a SHIFT, and from the SHIFT, it was evident that a transformation was taking place. The whole atmosphere of our church began to change. Our church began to grow. We grew by over three hundred people during this time and continued to grow for the next few years.

In March of 2020, we all remember what took place—COVID-19! God blessed us during the whole pandemic, and we recovered well. However, it seemed to me that we had entered into maintenance mode. We had bounced back strong, but now it appeared that our growth had stalled. In my time of prayer, the Lord began to deal with me again about the SHIFT. In my mind, I'm thinking, *Lord, we've already done that. I need something new!* As I went back and began to walk through all this material again, it felt as fresh now as it was the day God gave it to me. I realized that we were at this place again. We needed a SHIFT. The only difference was, we were at a different level now than we were in 2014.

Now, listen closely to what I'm about to tell you. Those of you who have read my book *HomeGrown*[26] know that my heart is for helping pastors grow churches in small-town rural communities. The point I want to make here is this: The tools that I have shared with you in this book are not bound by time, location, or church size. I have discovered that these principles will work in any location and in any-sized church. If you are averaging seventy-five, two hundred, six hundred, or a thousand, the SHIFT will always create an environment for a transformation.

---
26 Moore, *HomeGrown*.

We began implementing the SHIFT again, and the results have been the same. We are seeing the same things happening all over again that we experienced in 2014, just at a whole new level. The SHIFT is once again creating an environment for a transformation!

Many of you are probably thinking, *Okay, I hear you. But how do I go about implementing this? How do I create the SHIFT in my church?* I want to walk you through the process of creating a SHIFT and show you how all of this has worked for us. Let me warn you—I'm going to be very practical here, and I'm going to write this as if I were talking to you in a class.

We have looked at all five of these components individually: spiritual life, hospitality, interdependence, focus out, and transformation. Let's take another look at them and see how all the pieces fit together.

First of all, we must understand that a SHIFT doesn't happen overnight. It takes time and preparation for it to occur. This is probably the number one reason why most churches don't experience a SHIFT. Most pastors are looking for something that happens quickly. If you want to get your attendance up quickly, give away free ice cream at every service. But if you want to grow a church that will impact your town and your region, then read on.

# THE SHIFT

---

# IT IS THE PASTOR'S RESPONSIBILITY TO LEAD THE CHURCH INTO A PLACE WHERE A SHIFT CAN HAPPEN.

---

The SHIFT has to be centered around your mission and vision. The purpose of creating a SHIFT is to bring transformation to your church for the purpose of fulfilling your mission and vision. If you are unsure about the mission of your church, I would encourage you to read my book *HomeGrown*.[27] That book will help you in redefining the mission of your church by walking you through the entire process.

This SHIFT process starts with the pastor. It is the pastor's responsibility to lead the church into a place where a SHIFT can happen. One of the greatest tools and gifts that God has given us as pastors is the gift of preaching. If you want to cast vision, preach it. If you want to do something new, preach it. If you want to move your church forward, preach it. If you want to experience a SHIFT, preach it.

You should prepare a four-to-five-week series on each SHIFT component, starting with an introduction about the SHIFT. Use the material in this book. Take it, make it yours, and preach

---
27  Moore, *HomeGrown*.

it. At the end of this chapter, you will find a QR code where you can download sermon notes for the SHIFT series as well as other available series. Begin announcing the series a month in advance. You have to prepare your people for it. You have to begin telling your people that "Our church is about to experience a new beginning." You have to raise their expectation level. Tell them that "God is going to bring a SHIFT to our church that is going to transform us into a church that impacts our town!"

Don't be in a hurry to preach through the five components of the SHIFT. Don't just preach it and move on. For me, I would preach it on Sunday morning and teach it on Wednesday night. I would walk them through each component. I would schedule some meetings with my leaders and talk about how we could facilitate it. I would call them to commit to praying with me and walking with me on this journey. If they aren't interested in getting on board and making a commitment, I would begin looking for some new leaders.

## THE SPIRITUAL LIFE COMPONENT

The SHIFT always starts here, with the spiritual life component. Anytime you want to move your church and your people forward, this is always where it starts. You have to raise the spiritual climate of your people. I'm not trying to insult their intelligence, but act like they are new converts. Preach and teach as if they have never heard it before. Preach and teach them how to have a devotional life. Preach and teach on prayer. Teach them how to pray, what to pray, when to pray, and how long to pray. Preach and teach on worship. Preach and teach on spiritual gifts.

---

## OUR SERMONS ARE USELESS UNLESS WE SHOW THE PEOPLE HOW TO APPLY THEM.

---

You have to see this as a discipleship journey, not a revival. God has called us to be disciple-making pastors, and discipling people takes time. I am not against revival, but revivals do not make disciples. The only time that I personally have with the majority of my people is on Sunday morning. This is my opportunity to speak into their lives. I can't waste it away. I must be intentional with what I give them. My responsibility is to grow them up and move them forward in their relationship with God. I want to see them become fruitful in their lives and in a place of ministry. I want to teach them how to discover their purpose and how to live it out every day of their life. I want to teach them how to overcome obstacles that distract them from their purpose.

While it is imperative that you preach and teach through these components, it is just as important that you provide application for what you have preached. Many times, when we finish preaching and teaching through something, we move on to something else. We must provide our people with ways to apply it. Our sermons are useless unless we show the people how to apply them.

## THE HOSPITALITY COMPONENT

Applying the spiritual life component will naturally lead us into the hospitality component. Think about it. When you raise the spiritual climate in your congregation, people begin to love other people and begin to show themselves friendly at increased levels. The level of care rises as people become intentional about extending compassion to everyone who walks through the door.

At FWC, every time we ramped up our hospitality, our church grew. One way to ramp it up is through preaching and teaching. When was the last time you heard a sermon on hospitality? It has probably been a while! One of the most common things people who have stayed at FWC say is this: "This church was the friendliest church we have ever been to. They made us feel like they wanted us here." I am convinced that people do not know how to be hospitable. They have to be taught how to do it.

This is where hospitality gets a little complicated. You have to be strategic as to how you want to treat guests and develop a plan to get it done. You are going to have to meet with your leaders and volunteers and begin developing and training hospitality teams to implement the plan that you have put together. I laid all of this out in chapter 3. I would encourage you to go back to that chapter and work through the application process to develop a hospitality plan and put it to work.

## THE SHIFT

### THE INTERDEPENDENCE COMPONENT
Just like the spiritual life component leads into hospitality, the hospitality component leads right into the interdependence component. Effectively implementing the ministry of hospitality and all the other ministries of the church will require that all the parts of the body work together interdependently. Each part of the body has a role to play to ensure that "the whole body, being fitted and held together by what every joint supplies, according to the proper working of each individual part, causes the growth of the body for the building up of itself in love" (Ephesians 4:16).

---

## ONE OF THE MAIN REASONS VOLUNTEERS QUIT SERVING IS THAT THEY DON'T KNOW WHAT TO DO, AND THEY DON'T WANT TO LOOK STUPID.

---

Pastor, you're going to have to preach this and teach this for your people to get it. Trust me, at this point, they don't get it. If they did, they would be doing it. Like the other components, people have to be able to apply what you preach and teach. Your people need you to tell them what needs to happen and why. They want to know what you expect from them. Most of your people would be happy to help, but they need their leader to tell them what to do. One of the main reasons volunteers quit serving is that they don't know what to do, and they don't want to look stupid. They feel inadequate because they haven't been properly trained. Remember, this is what interdependence is all about.

My high school band director, Joe David, used to tell us, "We are only as strong as our weakest link." This is how it is in our churches too. Go back to chapter 4, and work through the application section with your people.

## THE FOCUS OUT COMPONENT

By now, you should be seeing some signs and feeling the tremors of a SHIFT arising! You are well on your way to experiencing a transformation. But, stay with me, we're not finished yet!

Up until now, your church was not ready to focus out. Think about it. Spiritually, we were not ready because we were focused on our own needs. Our hospitality was not up to par because we weren't expecting any new people to come. When it comes to interdependence, most of our people would have said, "What is that?" If fifteen new people had come to our church last Sunday, we would not have known what to do with them. But now! Now, we are ready for the focus-out component.

Like all the other components, we have to preach and teach it to our people. We cannot leave the harvest in the field—we must get it into the barn. We have to train our people to share their faith and be evangelistic. The key here is this: We are not trying to "do evangelism." We want to "be evangelistic." Jesus didn't do evangelism. He was evangelistic. People were attracted to Him. Truthfully, people are attracted to us. We must train our people to make the most of those who are in their lives every day. There are also those whom God strategically brings into our lives. We don't even have to search for them. All we have to do is lift up our eyes because the fields are ripe for harvest. If God brings them into our lives, then He has already given us favor to reach them.

Encourage your people to bring someone to church with them. Go back to chapter 5, and take your people through the application phase that I gave you. You're ready for this! You've been preparing your people, and the time is now. Be courageous and go get the harvest God has prepared for you and your church!

## THE TRANSFORMATION COMPONENT

The transformation component is the result of the first four. It's the stage of shifting gears into overdrive. When all four of the previous components are working, your church will begin to change from the inside out. You are now in a position for your mission to be realized. You begin to discover that you are living, loving, laboring, and lifting like God intended.

When the transformation component kicks in, it doesn't mean that your problems are over. What it means is that you will look at them differently and handle them with the wisdom and grace of God. What used to get you down now motivates you. You're excited to see what God will do this time. This is where you want to be. This is what happens when a divine SHIFT takes place.

But listen—the SHIFT doesn't happen by accident. It happens intentionally as we lead our church into a place where God's plan becomes our plan. When we work this plan, a SHIFT will occur, and it will always result in a church transformation.

# CONCLUSION

## CONCLUSION

As I bring this book to a close, I want to go back to where we started. We began by looking at Ezekiel's prophecy of *The Valley of the Dry Bones*. It was not a pretty sight. Quite frankly, it was pitiful. Bones lying all over the ground. Lifeless. Only a memory of what used to be. In my years of working with pastors, I have talked with many who have told me stories that sounded like Ezekiel's story. Their church is lifeless. They are discouraged. They have nothing left but a memory of what used to be. They are ready to give up and quit. Their hearts are broken as they contemplate leaving the ministry.

I wish I could say that that thought had never crossed my mind. But to be honest, I have considered it twice in my thirty-one years of ministry at FWC. The first time was just a few months before God gave me the SHIFT prophecy. The second time was when God took me back to the SHIFT prophecy. The message of this book saved my life and my ministry at FWC. I believe it could do the same for you.

God asked Ezekiel, "Can these bones live again?" When I read that story on that early July morning in 2013, I believe that God was asking me the same question that He asked Ezekiel. I must confess that my answer was the same as Ezekiel's. "Oh, Lord God, only you know!" God's answer was, "YES! They can live

# THE SHIFT

again!" What Ezekiel needed and what I needed was a SHIFT. I believe that's what you need too.

God is not finished with you, pastor! God is not finished with you, leader! God is not finished with you, businessman or businesswoman! Those bones can live again! Not only can they live again, but a SHIFT can cause breath to come back into them, and they can rise, stand on their feet, and become a mighty army.

The apostle Paul tells us:

> *But God, being rich in mercy, because of His great love with which He loved us, even when we were dead in our transgressions, made us alive together with Christ (by grace you have been saved), and raised us up with Him, and seated us with Him in the heavenly places in Christ Jesus. —Ephesians 2:4-6*

We see where God saved us when we were dead. He made us alive together with Christ. He raised us up with Him. He **seated** us with Him in heavenly places. What I see happening here in the New Testament with us is the same thing that happened to those bones in that valley in the Old Testament. There was a SHIFT that resulted in a transformation. We were dead. God saved us. He made us alive. He raised us up. He **seated** us with Him. He "locked us in" like a chain on a sprocket. He locked us in to fulfill a task.

*CONCLUSION*

You can build that church, pastor! If you will take the message of this book and put it into practice in your church, God will bring a SHIFT, and the SHIFT will bring to life that which was dead and cause it to stand up on its feet like a mighty army! God will bring transformation to your church!

I am also convinced that businessmen or businesswomen could take this same message and components and turn their business around. If you implement the principles in this book into your business, God will cause a SHIFT to happen in your business, and He will raise it from the dead, stand it on its feet, and cause it to arise as a mighty army.

So, here you go. The ball is in your court. It's your time for *The SHIFT: Creating an Environment for Transformation.*

"GROWING WHAT YOU HAVE, WHERE YOU ARE."

HOMEGROWN
PASTOR

WWW.HOMEGROWNPASTOR.COM

SCAN THE CODE NOW
TO START YOUR
JOURNEY WITH
HOMEGROWN PASTOR.

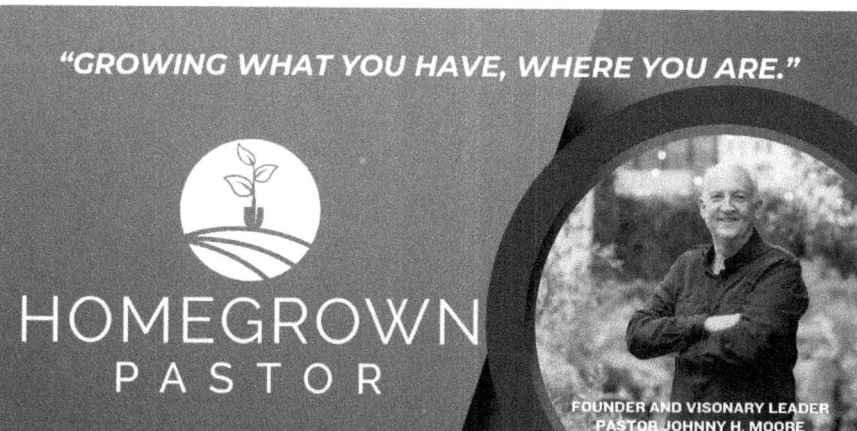

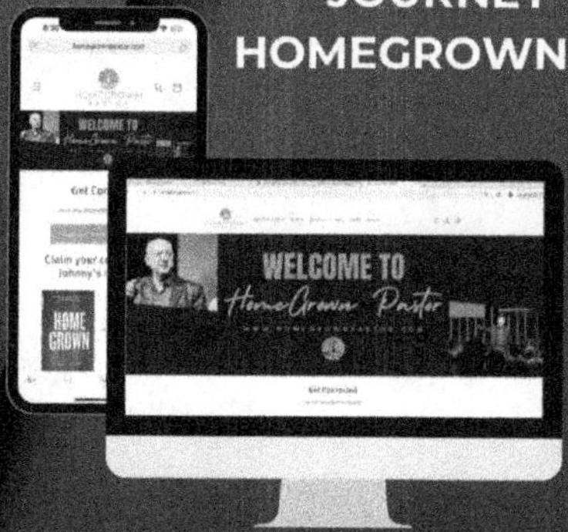


"HELPING SMALL TOWN PASTORS AND
LEADERS BUILD A GREAT CHURCH."

CONTACT US

229-377-8746

homegrownpastor.com

info@homegrownpastor.com

facebook.com/TheArtofAvail    @theartofavail

www.ingramcontent.com/pod-product-compliance
Lightning Source LLC
Chambersburg PA
CBHW070536090426
42735CB00013B/3000